JOY SHEFFIELD HARRIS

$\mathcal{A}$ Culinary History
of **FLORIDA**

Prickly Pears, Datil Peppers & Key Limes

AMERICAN PALATE

Published by American Palate
A Division of The History Press
Charleston, SC 29403
www.historypress.net

Cover: Key lime pie photographed by Joy Sheffield Harris. All other photographs courtesy of the State of Florida Memory Archives.

First published 2014
Second printing 2014

Manufactured in the United States

ISBN 978.1.62619.657.5

Library of Congress Cataloging-in-Publication Data

Harris, Joy Sheffield.
A culinary history of Florida : prickly pears, datil peppers and key limes / Joy Sheffield
Harris.
pages cm
Includes bibliographical references and index.
ISBN 978-1-62619-657-5 (paperback)
1. Food habits--Florida--History. 2. Food--Social aspects--Florida--History. 3. Cooking-
-Florida--History. 4. Cooking, American--Southern style. 5. Florida--Social life and
customs. I. Title.
GT2853.U5H37 2014
394.1'209759--dc23
2014032501

Contents

Acknowledgements

Thank you to the following people and places for their encouragement, inspiration and knowledge and to God for creating the Sunshine State and all its natural resources.

My husband, Jack, and our son, Jackson
My parents, Mary and Floyd Sheffield
Pat and Carolyn Sheffield
Dennis and Laurelyn Sheffield
Lisa Tamargo, for tasting and testing recipes
Rick and Ellen Nafe
Charles and LeAnn Knight
Marlene Forand
Cassie Jacoby
Joyce LaFray
Alyssa Pierce
Laura Reiley, *Tampa Bay Times*
Jeff Houck, *Tampa Tribune*
Thom Stork and Casey Coy, Florida Aquarium
Steve Koski and Dr. John Gifford, Little Salt Spring
Chris and Jr. Leitner, Swamp Cabbage Festival
Al and Patsy Berry, Plant City Strawberry Festival
The Gilberts, Creek Indian Trading Post, Panama City
Marcia McQuaig, Minorcan Datil Pepper Products

Ed and Beverly Pivacek, Putnam Lodge

Eric and Dee Hinshaw, Chalet Suzanne

Richard Bogey and Debbie Crosby, Florida's Natural Grove House

Dan Pirao, Bizarro Comics

Andrew T. Huse, for his Cuban sandwich demonstration

Preston Bozeman, Arthur Robinson and Paul Evans, for their flow of honey
and other details

Kathy Burnham, for her boiled peanuts

For sharing their school cafeteria memories: Kenn, Crook, Marja, Kathy,
Connie, Cindy, Slim, Sharon, David, Ruth, Luanne and Beverly

Southern Food Blogger friends: Jackie, Nicki, Virginia, Jessica, Pam, Lana,
Caroline and Andi

Janet Keeler and #CookClub friends at the *Tampa Bay Times*

True Florida Cracker Facebook friends

Mimi Reid Hardman, Historic Lake Wales Society

Tami Lee-Lanigan, Mission San Luis, Tallahassee

Sally Shifke, Henry B. Plant Museum, Tampa

1
Florida's First Cooks

The Sunshine State emerged from the sea as a group of islands, still submerged when dinosaurs roamed the nearby lands. It grew into a landmass twice its present size before developing into the recognizable peninsula that is Florida. Today's boundaries will be used to describe the unique culinary metamorphosis that took place in what was to become the Sunshine State. Full of rich natural resources and bountiful waters, Florida's landscape grew as tectonic plates shifted, making it the last geographical portion of the United States to fully develop. The much later discovery of *La Florida* by European explorers makes it the oldest settled land in the country. A shoreline extending more than fifty miles into the Gulf of Mexico, with temperatures below thirty degrees, was discovered by early inhabitants as they crossed a land bridge that existed where the Bering Sea is today. They migrated southeast and finally reached the Sunshine State, over twelve thousand years ago. The ice age ushered in the ancestors of Native Americans; these Paleoindians traveled in clans searching for food, bringing with them stone-age implements and the knowledge needed to hunt, gather and cook.

Following the food trail of large game, these nomadic hunters left their footprints on the Bering Strait as the ice age thawed and water submerged the pathway between the Americas and Asia. Coordinated activities with the animal kingdom were essential for survival, as the domestication of animals and agriculture were not yet practiced. Short-term camps were set up at kill sites for butchering and preparing meats for immediate consumption and storage for later use. Some of the largest animals known to man made up

Prehistoric man traveled in clans to hunt game with spears, as shown in this photograph of a drawing dated 1874.

their diet: saber-toothed cats weighing up to six hundred pounds, ground sloths twenty feet long, giant land tortoises and huge armadillos, along with mastodons and woolly mammoths. Bison, deer, llama and prehistoric wild horses were also a part of their diet, along with seeds, gourds and nuts, as determined by the interpretation of paleonutritionists.

Florida became wetter and warmer as big game began to disappear and the peninsula took shape. By then, these prehistoric people began to rely on smaller game and aquatic resources for survival. The sharing of food kept the clans together. Minimal and multipurpose cooking utensils—crafted of wood, bones, gourds, shells and stones—evolved along with the cooking process. Sticks and bones were used for stirring and holding foods over or near the fire; gourds and shells for carrying liquids; and larger stones for pounding meats and cracking bones. Flat stones were heated in and around the fire, and foods were cooked on the resulting hot surfaces.

Paleoindian sites, which submerged along the Inner Continental Shelf of the Gulf of Mexico and other areas (such as rivers, creeks, springs and sinkholes), are now home to thousands of artifacts. Harney Flats, in Hillsborough County, and Little Salt Spring, in Sarasota County, have yielded evidence that the once savannah-like areas were home to our most ancient ancestors, with multi-level artifacts from different eras serving as indicators revealing that others followed for thousands of years. These sites show that Paleoindians ate different seasonal diets in order to obtain adequate nutritional sustenance. Archaeological records reveal what the aboriginals ate and drank and how they caught, collected and prepared their foods. Zooarchaeologists and archaeobotanists help determine which natural resources were available and in which season they were utilized. Determining what aboriginals ate is easier than knowing how they prepared their meals.

Paleoindians settled near the mouths of rivers. Today, fossilized American mastodon remains provide information at some of these former watering holes: the Santa Fe River, Ichetucknee River, Aucilla River and Wacissa River, as well as Wakulla Springs, which at one time was only a dry cavern with a pocket of fresh water. The enormous size of these animals is more fully appreciated when you encounter their reconstructed skeletons at museums across Florida. Killing these large animals was a group effort, as was the cooking and preserving of the meat and skins. The meat had to be preserved because of the difficulty of acquiring food, and a variety of methods were later developed in order to secure a food supply year-round.

Little Salt Spring was most likely an oasis in a barren wasteland, used as a seasonal camp at the time of the Paleoindians. The sea-level ledge of the Paleoindian period is now eighty-five feet below the surface of the spring. Along with an oak mortar probably used for grinding nuts or seeds, one of the most intriguing finds was a now-extinct giant tortoise discovered upside down, impaled with a stake, over a charcoal pit, on a ledge eighty to ninety feet below the surface of the spring. The water level was even with the ledge twelve thousand years ago. Evidence gathered at the now-submerged site shows an informal hearth and charred remains, indicating man cooked at the site. Giant ground sloth, mammoth, bison and mastodon remains, as well as hickory nuts and gourd remains, were also found. One place on the underwater slope, before the deepwater drop-off, a series of stakes were driven into the ground, possibly a kind of trap for catching the abundant deer in the area. The culinary history of Florida is evidenced through the findings at places such as Little Salt Spring and Harney Flats.

When food is scarce, cultures adapt based on this need, whether it be through hunting, gathering, fishing or a combination of these methods. It most likely took thousands of years for the diet of early man to shift from the larger mammoths and mastodons of the cool and dry ice age to the deer, rabbits, fish, shellfish and wild plant foods of the warmer, wetter and more sedentary Archaic period. Acorns, hickory nuts, wild berries, sea grapes, cocoplums, prickly pears and persimmons became common dietary components in the new wet, warm environment. Glaciers were melting and sea levels rising, resulting in a decrease in the width of the state as the Gulf of Mexico and Atlantic Ocean drew nearer to present day levels. This also created more lakes, rivers, streams and ponds, making fresh water more readily available. Oak and hardwood trees emerged, and thousands of years later, pine and cypress swamps appeared, creating a Florida much like the one we see today. The changes in climate and landscape led to an easier way of life and a more nutritious diet. By adapting to these changes, the Florida Archaic Indians began to rely on a more varied diet, now dependent on fish, shellfish and plants, along with birds and other small game.

The beginning of the new Florida Archaic Indian lifestyle is marked by their use of the natural resources in the area to make knives and projectile points for hunting. The transition of the pieces from rough to smooth to polished reflect the Early, Middle and Late Archaic periods accordingly, with food-grinding implements ushering in the Early Archaic period. Milling stones and pottery, introduced toward the end of the Late Archaic period, helped create unique, separate cultures, or tribes, as they were later referred to during the Woodland period and the Mississippian period. Semipermanent settlements or camps turned into villages, and these villages were followed by the first permanent settlements of the Late Archaic period. Shell middens, also known as kitchen middens, along the Atlantic and Gulf coasts where food was prepared, eaten and discarded, reveal tools and charred remains that give us information about how food was killed, prepared and cooked. Shell middens and other camp artifacts are also located inland, near preferred sites for hunting and gathering.

The abundance of fresh water changed the living, cooking and eating habits of the Archaic people as they began to set up small camps when traveling to hunt for food and supplies. Year-round settlements along the coast, as well as ones near interior lakes, rivers and wetlands, provided a variety of fish and shellfish, along with other aquatic plants and animals, to enhance their diets. During this time, Lake Okeechobee and the Florida Everglades were formed, and Florida was beginning to look much like it does today, with its present-day sea levels and wooded areas. One factor in determining settlement locations was the need to stay close to fresh water sources. During the Middle Archaic period, hunters began to travel less as short- and long-term fish camps and other specialized seasonal hunting camps came into use. This is evidenced at locations such as Paynes Prairie.

This shell mound, or midden, was located in the Saint Petersburg area, where several mounds exist today.

Deer remains, found with large projectile points, indicate the animals were probably captured using these points. Impromptu dining at the scene of the hunt was no longer the norm, so the whole animal was taken back to the cooking area to be eaten. The Late Archaic period hunter upgraded from throwing sticks, clubs and spears to bows and arrows, blowguns, bolas and atlatls. A bola was a long cord with stones attached to each end. When thrown at a small animal, it would wrap itself around the prey, disabling it. The biggest improvement to hunting methods was the atlatl. Created to steady and lengthen the throwing arm, this wooden stick with a thong, or socket, would increase the effectiveness of the spear by greatly increasing its velocity, which in turn revolutionized hunting by making spears more deadly. While hunters traveled quietly through the woods in hopes of catching prey, they later used snares and traps that made hunting easier.

Sixteenth-century engravings by Theodor de Bry of 1564 drawings by the French artist Jacques le Moyne illustrate aboriginal hunters developing their own style. The alligator has survived millions of years, adapting to extreme temperature and environmental changes. One of the Bry engravings depicts an alligator being killed by ramming a long tree trunk down its throat and then flipping the alligator over and attacking it with bows and arrows, spears and clubs. Another shows aboriginal hunters who disguised themselves by wearing deerskins to which the

This 1500s depiction by Jacques le Moyne and Theodor de Bry shows an alligator being killed by ramming a tree trunk down its throat and flipping it over before attacking with bows and arrows, spears and clubs.

This 1500s depiction by Jacques le Moyne and Theodor de Bry shows Timucuan Indians hunting deer in disguise; notice the legs of the hunters under the deer on the left side.

heads were left attached. They would then ambush a deer and assault it with bows and arrows or darts hurled by an atlatl.

Fresh water may have determined where they lived, but the salt water, teeming with fish and shellfish, gave Florida Indians a variety of seafood. As subtropical conditions continued to emerge, marine resources became a larger part of the Archaic Indian diet. While still following the seasonal patterns of available foods, traveling to the coast and waterways for marine resources was necessary when the inland resources were depleted for the season. Coastal settlements were in part a result of the bounty of marine resources, where searching for food in the shallow waters of the Gulf of Mexico, rivers and streams was an easier way of life and a vast change for the Middle Archaic culture. Shell mounds, or middens, found along the coast indicate that huge amounts of fish and shellfish were consumed. Living in an estuary environment among the mangroves and buttonwood provided a vast amount of aquatic foods to the formerly mammal-based diet.

The Archaic Indians gathered shellfish by wading out into the shallow waters of barrier islands, bays and estuaries, or by waiting for the tide to fall. The catch might include conch, crab, clams, lobster, shrimp, fish and oysters. Oysters were a popular food item. Thriving where fresh water mixes with salt water, and attaching themselves to their surroundings, oysters could be loosened with a stick and carried off. No chase, no kill and the oyster could be eaten dead or alive, cooked or raw, right on the spot or dried for later use. Oysters were abundant, and from the quantity of discarded oysters shells found in middens throughout the state of Florida, it appears the Archaic Indians and those who followed found them to be a perfect "fast food." They might have discovered by accident one of the easiest cooking methods. Fresh oysters, when placed on hot coals or fire, open spontaneously and if left on the coals a little longer, become roasted oysters.

Men did most of the fishing, first with clubs and then spears and hooks and lines, later improving their chances further by creating nets and traps. The fish gorge, used for thousands of years, later evolved into the fishhook. Fishing is believed to have begun in rivers and lakes, before anglers ventured out into the Gulf of Mexico and Atlantic Ocean in boats or dugout canoes. These canoes were first used by the Middle Archaic Indians and have been found in several locations around Florida. The canoes were not only used for fishing but were also a major mode of transportation. They were used to travel from Fort Myers to Lake Okeechobee on the Caloosahatchee River, referred to as the canoe highway.

Tidal traps or fishing weirs were likely used to catch larger fish in greater quantities. When the fish swam over the fence in high tide, the weir caught them as the tide went out.

As fishing techniques improved, so did the Paleoindian diet. Spear throwers caught eels and turtles. Smaller fish, such as mullet, pinfish, catfish and pigfish, were netted using cordage (made from twisted palm or other plant fibers). Tidal traps or fishing weirs were likely used to catch larger fish in greater quantities. The fish weir was a wooden or reed fence that stretched across a stream or river to trap or catch fish. When the fish swam over the fence in high tide, the weir caught them as the tide went out. Another process along the same principle, used for catching fish, was damming, where upright stakes or laced branches were placed in streams.

Sea grapes and cocoplums grew wild in the area. Botanically speaking, sea grapes are not related to the cultivated grapes we find at the market but are similar in some ways. The fruits are reddish to purple and hang in clusters like grapes, but the individual grapes within a cluster do not all ripen at the same time and need to be picked one at a time from the cluster. Today often seen as an ornamental shrub along coastal areas of Florida, sea grapes are also used for making wine or jelly.

Late Archaic Indians were mound builders as well as midden producers, building three types of mounds: a burial mound, a platform mound for temples or other buildings and a kitchen midden or shell mound. The kitchen midden is a place where prehistoric man disposed of his kitchen waste, such as shells and bones, to keep living areas free from debris. This continued for hundreds of years, producing huge mounds. Some middens consist mostly of shells and are so large that they can still be seen today. Located on the Canaveral National Seashore, Turtle Mound is the tallest shell midden in the United States; in prehistoric times, it measured more than seventy-five feet high. This mound was so large that the early Spanish explorers used it as a landmark when navigating the area.

In *The Rituals of Dinner*, Margaret Visser states, "Civilization can not begin until a food supply is assured," and the entire state of Florida was a region full of aboriginal activity. Today, traces of Archaic and Paleoindian habitats are found in unassuming neighborhoods, usually near water sources. Much of the information about what they ate comes from the kitchen middens left behind. Archaeobotanical identification reflects floral and faunal remains found at prehistoric sites around the state. These gatherers used a systematic method when searching for insects, eggs, shellfish and edible plants. They searched for edible plants such as prickly pears cactuses, berries, nuts and roots (from starchy sources such as the coontie and bulrush).

Florida's state tree, the sabal palm—more commonly referred to as the cabbage palm—and the saw palmetto provided a source of nutrition to the earliest Floridians and is still used today for nutritional and medicinal purposes. Plant remains are not as well preserved in middens, but based on the information available, it appears that many calories from plants were consumed.

While gathering food for the group, foraging along the way provided additional nutritional substance to the diet of aboriginals. Why men hunted and women gathered is still in debate, but one thought is that women tend to be more patient, as gathering is an ongoing process, and men tend to be more aggressive. Growing vegetables takes time and effort, without the excitement and intensity of hunting. In *Catching Fire*, British primatologist Richard Wrangham makes the comparison of "women digging roots and men hunting meat in one culture, or women shopping and men earning a salary in another." Thus, the genders have made different but complementary contributions to the household for thousands of years.

Still, the hunter depended on the gatherer in the event he came back empty-handed. Women gathered from the wooded areas and waterways and were also in charge of preparing and serving the meals. Children and the elderly assisted in gathering. A typical day might find the men off to hunt for deer, small mammals or birds, while the women and children roamed in search of other sources of nutrition. While the hunters needed quickness, agility and stamina, the gatherers had to have the ability to determine which plants or herbs were edible, as well as knowing the uses of the various plant

Hunters and gatherers. *Copyright 2002 Bizarro Comic, courtesy of Dan Piraro.*

parts. Understanding the life cycle of plants and the seasonal variations was crucial to providing an adequate and edible diet.

Many of the wild edibles our ancestors enjoyed are still around today but are often overlooked as a basic source of nutrition. From the roots to the leaves, if it was edible, they ate it. And if it wasn't, they figured out how to remove the toxins and then use it as a food source. For example, pokeweed, also known as pokeberry, poke, poke salat or poke salad, is often referred to when referencing wild greens; however, the plant is toxic and has to be prepared properly before it is eaten. (Wild plants for consumption should be collected with knowledge and caution.) Coontie, what was later called

Florida arrowroot, was still being harvested as a staple starch and processed to remove toxins many years later by Native American tribes in Florida, as well as the early pioneers.

The origin of cooking food goes back beyond the time of the Paleoindians in Florida. As Wrangham writes, "One of the great transitions in the history of life, stemmed from the control of fire and the advent of cooked meals," and "the breakthrough of using fire…would have been the biggest culinary leap," leading to better ways of preparing foods. Some foods are naturally tender and delicious, but cooking makes our food safer and more palatable. Cooking also increases the nutritional value of food by changing the chemical composition, making foods easier to chew and digest and facilitating the absorption of proper nutrients, at the same time eliminating harmful toxins and bacteria. Along with the advantage of reducing spoilage, cooking creates rich, delicious flavors. In order to have better-tasting foods, the hunters of past generations learned, through trial and error, that an animal captured and killed without a chase meant better-tasting meat. Naturally, meat flavors are enhanced when the animal is calm at the moment of slaughter, as this calmness helps to retain more glycogen in the muscle, which converts to lactic acid when slaughtered, resulting in tender meat and a much more delicious meal.

The Paleoindians spent most of their time acquiring food and making sure they had enough to survive, rather than spending time trying to make it more palatable. However, cooking did that naturally by changing the chemical composition of the foods via browning or carmelization. Known as the Maillard reaction, this changed the flavor for the better. The browning of foods through high heat created new, richer flavors, and sizzling food over an open flame helped to bring out these natural flavors. Cooking over a campfire was a primitive way of producing better-tasting and more nutritious foods through chemistry. Taste and tenderness become more important once the food supply is regulated and one can spend more time refining the flavors of the dishes. As early man foraged after a brush fire, he might have discovered some of the first roasted seeds and nuts. Another accidental discovery might have occurred in cooler areas. When animal carcasses were found after several days, the meat would be tenderized, allowing for better-tasting cooked food, similar to the meat-locker process used today.

Using seasonal ingredients, Archaic Indians adapted both their eating habits and cooking styles to incorporate new foods and cooking methods. Men were often off hunting all day. The women of the village usually had food prepared in case the men came back empty-handed or to supplement what was caught. The men and boys might bring along something to eat during the day, such as dried meat. One convenience food of the past still eaten today is jerky. These thin pieces of lean meat were dried over a fire of non-resinous wood or in the sun and wind. As the meat loses most of its water content, it becomes hard and dark. The fire doesn't cook the meat; it just allows for the heat and smoke to speed up the drying process. Today, you can find beef, buffalo, gator and venison jerky at grocery stores and roadside stands all around Florida. As the indigenous people of Florida roamed about, they carried jerky along with them for a snack. Aboriginal people carried pemmican, made by pounding the dried meat to a powder and then adding bear fat, along with fruits or nuts when available.

Before farming techniques were introduced, seasonality of foods played a major role in their diet. Both seafood and plant foods were seasonal. In some parts of the state, during warm weather, fish and shrimp were plentiful, while the cold weather yielded hard clams and oysters. They could all be enjoyed year-round when preserved by smoking and drying. The early method of smoking meat by placing the meat or fish next to the fire, draped over sticks, was a long, slow process. Many of our modern smoked products are prepared for immediate consumption only, and the smoking process is used to enhance the meat's flavor and does not preserve the food. When food is smoked at home, it is usually brined first, and the finished product still needs refrigeration.

A variety of nuts, such as hickory and acorn, gathered in the fall and winter were used for making breads (by grinding them into flour), as flavoring in soups and stews or as a source for oil or "nut butters" used in cooking. Acorns can be bitter, astringent and toxic. If used to make acorn cakes or mush, tannins and other impurities were first leached from the nuts through a simple process. One method was to place the nuts in a basket and set it in a stream for a few weeks. Another method was to bury the nuts in the swamp and then dig them up before they germinated. Sometimes the nuts were shelled, ground and buried in hot, moist ground to leach out the bitter tannin and toxins. Ground acorns could then be used as a meal to thicken stews, make bread or as a beverage.

The Archaic people created a new tool called a nutting stone. A large, flat stone with several indentations carved in it held the nuts in place before they were pounded with another stone and the nutmeat was removed. Some nuts were dried, then pounded with a mortar and pestle and mixed with water for a broth-like mixture to drink or cook with. Now that these people's lifestyles were sedentary, they could afford to keep heavy stone tools around to use when cooking.

Wooden implements, such as a mortar and pestle, also changed the food preparation style of early man, but it was the development of pottery that brought about the biggest changes to cooking and storing food. Discoveries of ancient pottery allow archaeologists to determine time periods and establish regional groups based on different pottery styles. With foods more readily available, they probably ate whenever they were hungry, unless they had a system within the village for daily preparation of food. At times, men might eat only one daily meal in the evening. They ate more when they had more. The women and children could stop along the way while foraging to eat some of what they gathered, such as native plants, nuts or berries. As food became easier to acquire, breakfast consisted of leftovers from the previous day's supper.

"We can learn to be cooks, but we must be born knowing how to roast," wrote Jean Anthelme Brillat-Savarin in 1825. This quote is most applicable to the progression of cooking style of our ancient ancestors. Cooking meat by laying it directly on hot coals was the easiest and most likely method of cooking the catch of the day. Prehistoric man usually cooked big game whole or in large slabs to serve the entire community. This was done soon after the catch, and eating occurred when foods were available without regard for breakfast, lunch or dinner. Surplus meat dried by the fire would be kept for later use. Smaller animals could be cooked whole, with the hide acting as a protective barrier.

During the Archaic era, skewers were wedged between rocks or boulders and held over the flame to cook slowly, freeing up the cook to perform other tasks. By skewering large quantities of meat on a stick wide enough to extend across the fire pit, the food could then be laid across the pit and turned as necessary, the precursor to the spit.

Culinary options for early Floridians increased as different cultures developed cooking styles suitable to the environment, thus creating different and practical cuisines. Tools and utensils used for preparing and cooking meals were improving as well. Stones, shells, wood, bones and teeth were used either as utensils themselves or to create new utensils. Sharp teeth or stones were inserted into a board to be used as a scraper for grating roots and tubers. Sharkskin was used as sandpaper, while some animal stomachs, dried hides and dried gourds were used as containers for storage and cooking. Many shellfish came with their own containers for cooking, as did turtles. Keeping live turtles tethered via perforations in their shells until ready to eat was another practice for storing food.

Some of the first cooking enhancements were heated stones and earth ovens. In order to heat liquid, in containers such as animal stomachs or hides, "boiling stones" were heated in the fire and then placed in the container or a pit to cook the contents. Boiling stones and earth ovens were used to prepare a larger array of foods. Animal hides were used as lids to keep in the heat. Other oven-like methods were used by mixing coals and sand and then burying the food within. Archaic Indians experimented with times and types of foods. Wrapping foods with green leaves to keep the dirt and ashes out led to more experimenting with advanced cooking techniques. Earth ovens consisted of various sizes of pits dug near the fire, filled with embers or hot stones for baking. Covering loaves of bread (made from roots or other starches) with leaves helped to protect them from the warm ashes and coals placed on top of them while cooking. Heated clay balls of various sizes were placed inside earth ovens for baking as well. These clay balls were first dried by heat before being used to assist in baking, roasting or boiling. To boil and steam food, cooking pits were lined with overlapping stones or animal hides to prevent seepage. In some instances, the cooking ovens or pits were filled with refuse after meals and covered or burned. As a precursor to pottery, in clay soil, the inner fire would bake the sides of the pit into an earthenware lining and possibly a waterproof cooking pit. Large permanent stone pots were also created with fires built around the pot. Later, pottery or waterproof pouches of hides or innards were hung over the fire to simmer foods.

Feast or famine was the "special of the day," while hunting, gathering, fishing, foraging, picking, plucking, digging, searching and scrounging were methods of food procurement long before farming became a natural means to a steady food supply.

Florida's First Farmers and Tribes[2]

With the dawn of agriculture on the horizon, the Neolithic Revolution—a term coined by Australian archaeologist V. Gordon Childe—ushered in the domestication of plants and animals, and cultures flourished. Just as thousands of years of climate change brought the melting of glaciers and stabilized sea levels, which in turn created the ideal environment for fast-growing plants, "People were not foragers one day and farmers the next. Indeed, agriculture and animal husbandry took many millennia to establish," writes Michael Symons in his 2004 book, *A History of Cooks and Cooking*. Incipient agriculture was the antecedent to civilization, occurring independently and at different times in different parts of the world. When man realized a seed dropped along the way turned into an ear of corn with the help of sunshine, soil and water, he was on the path to a more settled lifestyle. By the Late Archaic period, Native Americans knew when to sow and when to reap, becoming the first farmers of the land. Collecting useful plant parts began the process of tending, which was later followed by weeding and pruning. The first domesticated plants in America were cucurbits, which include a variety of climbing plants such as squash, pumpkins, cucumbers, gourds, watermelons and cantaloupes. Sunflowers, sweet potatoes, chili peppers and papayas would soon follow. Maize, also known as corn, would eventually become the dominant crop of North America. Around 1500 BC, agriculture began to spread across America. By 1000 BC, the art of growing corn began to improve the diet and lives of the post-Archaic Indians.

Previously moving seasonally, these fully developed cultures were more inclined to stay longer in one place to till the soil and nurture the gardens. They coalesced into villages, establishing permanent settlements in every part of the state. Improved diets resulted in population increases and larger villages as distinctive native cultures settled down and societies developed complex social structures. An abundant variety of food filled the forests and waters, including bear, deer, turkey, waterfowl, nuts and berries, along with a staggering variety of fish and shellfish. Like the alligator, some plants such as turnips, radishes and onions had survived for millions of years in the wild. To be able to plant the crop of their choice was a big change for these early Floridians.

The foundation of early farming communities, along with continent-wide trade connections, improved nutrition for Florida Indians. In North Florida, the main crops harvested were maize, beans, squash, pumpkins, melons and sunflowers, the most important crop being maize. With the right environment and fertile soil, corn was simple to grow: Poke a hole in a hill of dirt, plant the seeds and remove the weeds. Corn could be planted alongside beans and squash using the intercropping method, an improvement over the slash-and-burn method. Many Native Americans still used a cleared-field farming technique in the spring by cutting down the trees and setting the field on fire to clear away remaining debris and weeds. The ash added nutrients to the soil. After hoeing the field, seeds were planted in small hills of dirt. Corn was usually planted by women using a coa, or digging stick, after first soaking the corn in water to soften it. After a few years, the soil would be exhausted, and they would move to a new area.

Corn, beans and squash are often referred to as the "three sisters" or the "trinity," since they complemented one another in the ground and on the table. Beans grew up the corn stalks, which acted as a trellis, and helped to stabilize the corn stalk, utilizing less space, with the squash growing under the shade of the corn plant. The squash plants helped to shade the shallow roots of the corn and hold in moisture. Nitrogen from the bean roots helped to nourish the corn.

Just as the Paleoindians came in search of new food sources, in 1492 Christopher Columbus, in his quest for Asiatic spices, led to the accidental discovery of the Spice Islands and European exploration of the Americas. The Columbian Exchange, as described by environmental historian Alfred Crosby, brought about "the greatest biological revolution in the Americas since the end of the Pleistocene era," with an exchange of new foods between the Old World and the New World. When Columbus arrived, corn was widely eaten raw, boiled, roasted or ground.

This 1500s depiction by Jacques le Moyne and Theodor de Bry shows the men tilling the soil and the women using a coa, or digging stick, for planting.

Tomatoes made their first appearance as weeds in prehistoric times, but eventually tomatoes, potatoes, avocados, pineapples, beans, chocolate, peanuts, vanilla, peppers and turkey made their way from Central and South America to the tribes of Florida. Honey is frequently mentioned in association with Native Americans in Florida, but it wasn't until the 1770s that honey became more common across the state. In 1775, Bernard Romans wrote *A Concise Natural History of East and West Florida* and mentioned honey in the area, stating, "It is of so good a quality, as in my opinion to exceed that of Calabria and Minorca."

Improved food sources, storage and cooking techniques, along with the introduction of pottery, had a significant influence on the way native Indians prepared food, resulting in more nutritious options. Regional cooking was born out of the need to utilize foods available in certain locations and seasons. Some natives cultivated the soil, while others hunted, fished or gathered roots and berries. Others used a combination of ways to feed themselves, living in close communion with the natural environment. Along the coast, aquatic resources—including whales, seals, rays and manatees—played a major part in supplying nutritional subsistence, even more so farther south. Common foods throughout the state were deer, turtles, birds, bears, raccoons,

Photographed in 1937 by Herman Gunter, this ancient clay water bottle was retrieved from a Hillsborough County archaeology project.

opossum, rabbits, snakes and wild edibles.

Along with farming, hunting, fishing and gathering, these communities depended on seasonal bounty and worked in harmony with nature. Planting in the spring, they depended on aquatic resources or woodland gathering to sustain themselves until the fall harvest was ready. Farming had a way of unifying cultures, especially in North Florida. Native Florida Indians experienced a population explosion, and hundreds of tribes of all sizes were spread out across the state. European explorers gave regional cultures and small tribes alike some of the more common names associated with Florida history, such as Timucua, Apalachee, Choctaw, Creek, Tocobaga, Calusa, Ais, Jeaga, Tequesta and Matecumbe.

Shells, sticks and stone blades were originally used for cooking and preparing food but later gave way to carved wooden spoons and fired clay pottery. Early inhabitants of Florida also used animal skins and stomachs, gourds, wood and bamboo to make multi-use baskets or containers. "Inland Floridians along the St. Johns River boiled their food in large Gulf Coast Whelk shells," writes Robin Brown in *Florida's First People*. A mortar and pestle or nutting stone was used to grind nuts to make mush. As cooking became more advanced, these early inhabitants created knives by polishing bone, and drank from gourds and shell cups. Food was protected in woven baskets, clay pots or wrapped in animal skins. From the woodland areas to the agricultural fields, and from the Gulf Coast to the Atlantic Ocean, some of the foods prepared by Florida's first cooks are still echoed in the foods we eat today.

While there are no recipes or cookbooks to describe what the indigenous people of Florida cooked and ate, there are ethnographic and archaeological records, which give us a vast source of information to deduce how the prehistoric inhabitants of Florida might have survived. In his book *Florida's Indians from Ancient Times to the Present,* Jerald T. Milanich described an excavated site near Paynes Prairie that revealed a diet of at least ten species of fish, as well as snails and clams, seven species of birds, five species of shark and a variety of other foods sources. Rookeries were also raided for young birds and eggs.

An early Native American site in North Florida produced artifacts that indicated a hearth within the house was used for cooking, writes Milanich in *Life in a 9th Century Indian Household: A Weeden Island Fall-Winter Site on the Upper Apalachicola River, Florida.* Pits found in and around the house held charred remains of bones and tools such as scrapers, choppers, projectile points, knives, grinding stones and boiling stones, while others were possible storage pits. Some of the pits might have been for support beams for drying or smoking racks, others for steaming in a style similar to a clambake. A large number of quartz river rocks were found at the site; the surfaces were burnt, indicating their use as boiling or baking stones.

Fire-stable pottery improved the diet of early Native Americans by allowing a combination of foods to be cooked together in a stew over direct heat, combining meat, fowl and fish with fruits and vegetables for a more nutritious and flavorful meal. One of the easiest ways to prepare a meal was to put it all in one big stew pot made from animal parts or pottery. At first placed directly in the fire, the stew pot was later elevated on three stones above the fire. This saved time and energy since all ingredients were cooked at the same time over a smaller heat source. This provided an easy way to have food ready to eat all day long while attending to other chores.

Native Americans smoked corn, meats (cut into thin strips) and fish using a slow process that sterilized and dehydrated the foodstuff, making it safe to eat for weeks. A barbacoa, a wooden frame (built of green wood so it did not burn) with vertical poles holding a grid above a smoky fire, was often used. This was the precursor to the barbecue grill we use today. Another process used small huts with hickory or oak wood fires within that were constantly burning.

The first written sources of information about Florida's early Indian tribes comes from records kept by European explorers. In the early 1500s, when Spanish explorers first arrived in Florida, they encountered the Timucua in northeast and central Florida; the Apalachee, Choctaw and Creek in the Panhandle; the Tocobaga in Tampa Bay; the Calusa in southwest Florida; Ais, Jeaga and Tequesta in southeast Florida; and the Matecumbe in the Florida Keys.

This 1500s depiction by Jacques le Moyne and Theodor de Bry shows a barbacoa used for drying fish, small animals and other foods.

In his *Historical Collections of Louisiana and Florida*, B.F. French wrote, "The Southern Indians were, in general, great gourmands, and lived sumptuously on wild game, fish, and oysters, buffalo, deer and bear-meat in their season. They also freely ate corn, beans, pumpkins, and persimmons, of which they made bread mixed with corn-meal." French goes on to say that the variety of fish included some that were new to European explorers—such as trout, mullet, perch and bass—and that the Indians dined on mulberries, raspberries, honey, venison, grapes, maize, citrons, cucumbers, peas, roots, herbs, mussels, crabs, lobsters and beans with fish. War and disease led to the demise of most of the aboriginal Indians.

The Native Americans living in Florida today are not the same Indians who lived in Florida thousands of years ago, but the Creek, Miccosukee and Seminole have called Florida home for hundreds of years. European explorers found the Apalachee around the area today known as Leon and Jefferson Counties, with the Choctaw and Creek farther west across the Panhandle. Highly successful and organized farmers growing corn, beans, peas, squash, pumpkins and sunflowers, they also dined on aquatic resources from the lakes, ponds, marshy areas and the Gulf of Mexico. They also ate inland animals such as bear, deer, fox, opossum and raccoon. As part of the Mississippian culture, they built hundreds of platform mounds with plazas and villages, some still existing today at Fort Walton Beach and Lake Jackson Mounds State Archaeological Site, just north of Tallahassee. The Lake Jackson site was built between 1200 and 1500 AD and was the capital of the Apalachee Province.

Maize, later called Indian corn by the British, was the most important crop. It was planted in rows and stored in tribal granaries or in a common-house that was situated by a stream for easy access or by a hillside for shade. They also stored dried fruit, roots and nuts along with dried and smoked meats. Some food was stored in deep floor pits lined with hides or grass. At times, a "pahas" was used, which is a small storage house, perhaps sealed with mud, to hold corn, dried meat and other foods for the winter. The chief had a special granary to disperse foods, as he felt was needed.

Colder parts of the state were planted in only once a year, while some of the warmer regions yielded crops twice a year. In the warmer areas, halfway

This 1500s depiction by Jacques le Moyne and Theodor de Bry shows the harvest being brought to a common-house or food storage unit, also known as a granary, situated by a stream for easy access.

through the summer, the ripe "early corn" was picked and eaten along with squash, pumpkins, sunflowers and beans. Another late corn crop was harvested in the fall. The summer corn was eaten raw or boiled, but the autumn corn was dried and stored for the winter to be used as seeds. It was also husked, shelled and dried and then pounded into grits or cornmeal with large wooden mortars and pestles. Added to stews or made into gruel, the cornmeal was also mixed with water and fried in bear grease to make corncakes.

The women, in addition to gathering and cooking, also tended the gardens and made baskets, utensils and pottery. They used shells and gourds to make the baskets and utensils. Fruits and berries were collected and dried for a few days in the sun. Extracts from fermented fruits, berries, barks and roots were used, along with other herbs and spices, in cooking. Nut oils and bear grease were common cooking ingredients. Crushed nuts were boiled in water, and once cooled, the oil could be skimmed from the top of the liquid. Other preparation methods included mixtures of crushed acorn and dried corn pounded together and made into a mush. A variety of foods were made into breads using acorns, beans, berries, nuts, onions, peas, persimmons, squash and sweet potatoes.

The Creek from Georgia and Alabama brought to Florida a legacy that is still around today. One of their common food practices was the way they prepared hickory milk, a staple ingredient. They pounded the shelled, dried hickory nuts and then boiled the nutmeat in water. It was then strained, and the oily part that was left was like cream. The knowledge of how to use plants for food sources is remarkable when you consider flour was being made from cattails and acorns long before wheat flour was introduced in the state. The common cattail provides fine flour made from the bright yellow pollen, and the rootstock provides nutritious starch.

A Choctaw favorite was sassafras, with its root beer aroma, which they shared as a part of the Columbian Exchange. The aromatic bark, roots and leaves were used as beverages and for flavoring other dishes. Dried sassafras leaves were powdered and added to stews to thicken and flavor them, much like filé powder is used today for gumbos and Creole cookery. For tea, the leaves were muddled and steeped, or the dried roots and bark were steeped in boiling water for a longer period of time. Today, caution is given for using wild sassafras, as the stems and roots can be toxic.

Although they had many foods in common, each tribe was unique and had a diet that reflected the specific areas in which it lived. The Timucua were a group of Indians from the northeast coast and central part of Florida, likely the first group to come in contact with European explorers. Timucua villages were located near rivers, swamps, inland forests or along the coast. Although the Timucua were not intensive farmers like the Apalachee, archaeological records show they started cultivating maize around 750 AD, in the Saint Johns River region. Crops of corn, beans, squash and pumpkins were usually planted in fields near villages, but the type of soil had something to do with the placement of gardens. For instance, since the soil east of the Saint Johns River was sandy, the gardens were smaller than those on the west side, where excellent crops grew due to the rich soil there.

In addition to planting crops, the Timucua hunted wild game in the forest and swamps, using handmade spears, bows and arrows, clubs and blowguns to kill their game. Seasonal sites along the coast were used to gather and process (remove the shells and dry or smoke) clams, oysters and fish to supplement their meat and agricultural diet. This resulted in the large shell mounds along the coasts, some of which can still be seen today. Snails gathered from the Saint Johns River were a staple food of the tribe.

On Florida's Gulf Coast, the Tocobaga of the Tampa Bay area left many shell mounds, demonstrating the fact that several Native American groups were living in small villages along Tampa Bay, with the main village near Safety Harbor. A temple mound, in Philippe Park in Safety Harbor, on Tampa Bay can still be seen today. From 900 to 1500, the Tocobaga relied heavily on the abundant resources from the bay area, including fish and shellfish that they easily collected. They hunted and gathered wild plants, nuts, berries and fruits to supplement their diets. As great hunters, they enjoyed eating deer, rabbits, armadillos, squirrels, turkeys, raccoons and manatees as part of their diet. Agricultural evidence suggests they planted corn as well, but it contributed very little to their diet.

The Calusa, of the southwest Gulf Coast area to Lake Okeechobee, were great sailors and fishermen. They lived a coastal life, and this maritime group of fierce warriors used the Caloosahatchee River as their inland highway, relying on the freshwater resources of the interior, as well as fish and shellfish along the coast, for their daily diet. Although they were not agriculturists, they depended on the estuaries for food and kept small gardens as an added food source. In the northern and central part of the state, the soil was better suited to the practice of agriculture and yielded more rewarding results than the sandy soil along the coasts and in South Florida.

The main staple food was both fresh- and saltwater fish and shellfish. Whelks and conch were eaten in large quantities, as were quahog clams. The Calusa also supplemented their diet with small game, deer and turtles.

Plant food consumed in the area included cabbage palm, saw palmetto berries, cocoplums, hog plums, sea grapes, prickly pears, squash, acorns and roots (for making bread). Even papaya and chili peppers were possibly utilized, as indicated by findings at the Pine Island site. At one time, there was a Calusa mullet fishery called Tanpa (With an 'n' not to be confused with Tampa). Situated where Pineland is today, at the mouth of Charlotte Harbor, the harbor was originally named Bahia de Tanpa, as shown on a 1683 map drawn by a Spaniard named Alonso Solana. Tampa, to the north, erroneously received the name when another cartographer inaccurately located the harbor on his map. Today, Pineland and Mound Key are the two largest Calusa shell mound sites in the area and are considered former Native American towns.

The Calusa used wood, shells and fish bones for utensils such as dippers, cups and spoons, as well as for making spears for fishing and hunting. A variety of nets, such as dip, gill, stop and seine nets, were made for fishing, along with other fishing tools like spears, hooks, gorges, weirs and traps. Rawhide, sinew and gut were used for making ropes that then could be used to attach handles to tools. The men hunted small game and deer while the women and children collected shellfish and gathered plants, fruits, roots and nuts. Many lived in chickees—shelters without walls made from cypress logs for support of the palm frond, thatched, waterproof roofs. The Spanish described houses with doors and windows, as well as miles-long canals, dug by hand, used for easier transportation.

South of Cape Canaveral and into the Florida Keys lived many tribes along the coast, including the Ais, Jeaga (also known as the Jega, Jobe or Hobe) and Tequesta with the Matecumbe in the Florida Keys. These South Florida tribes were not agricultural people but were hunters and gatherers of mostly marine life, including sharks, sailfish, porpoises and manatees. The Ais lived from Cape Canaveral to Fort Pierce, near the Indian River Inlet in villages. They used dugout canoes tied together to go out into the ocean. Fishing along the Indian River lagoon and in the Atlantic Ocean served as a major food source for the Ais, along with inland hunting.

Opposite, top: South Florida tribes were not agricultural people but were hunters and gatherers of mostly marine life, including shark, sailfish, porpoises and manatees.

Opposite, bottom: Sea grapes, a food popular among indigenous tribes, are still a part of the coastal landscape of Florida. *Photographed by world-renowned photographer Joseph Janney Steinmetz.*

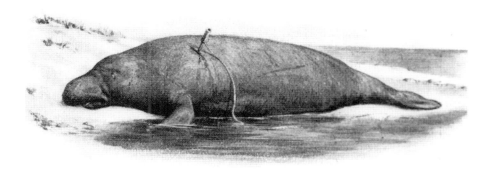

The Tequesta of Biscayne Bay considered the manatee a special food, served only to the most important leaders of the tribe, as it was thought to be very tasty. The Matecumbe, who occupied the Florida Keys as far back as AD 800, were known for eating whales, turtles, crayfish, snails, deer, bears, mako sharks and swordfish. They also collected clams, conches, oysters and turtle eggs, along with nuts, palm berries, cocoplums, cabbage palm, saw palmetto and sea grapes.

Many of these Atlantic coast native tribes gained fame from *Jonathan Dickinson's Journal*, written circa 1699, in which he recalled how he, along with his family and others, survived a shipwreck on the southeast coast of Florida. They depended on these tribes for their survival as they tried to make their way to Saint Augustine and eventually farther north. According to Dickinson, these people "neither sow nor plant any manner..." but did, on occasion, offer bitter palmetto berries and fish. Not to their liking, these dark, olive-shaped palmetto berries "tasted of rotten cheese steeped in tobacco," and the fish was "boiled with scales, head and gills..." Cocoplums and sea grapes were found along the way, but the variety of food was limited for these shipwrecked survivors.

The first farming in Florida included the cultivation of corn, beans, squash and pumpkins. Corn played an important role in the diet and lives of every early American, from the Natives to the Crackers. Early settlers learned preparation techniques that Native Americans had perfected hundred of years earlier. Native Americans also introduced new words such as "succotash," "squash," "opossum," "hickory," "pecan," "raccoon," "cougar" and "hominy." The gastronomic excitement continued to flourish as various cooking methods were developed in order to incorporate new foods into native diets.

3
Viva la Florida and the First Thanksgiving

La Florida, meaning "feast of the flower," is the beautiful Spanish name given to the peninsula and a large portion of southeastern North America by Juan Ponce de León over a half a millennium ago. He, and the European explorers who followed, did more than unveil new lands. They created a foundation for a "feast of the foods" by planting the seeds for the agriculture, fishing and cattle industries in Florida. The early Spanish explorers and settlers had a profound impact on the distribution of new crops in the New World. Although very little was recorded concerning eating habits, cooking and foods of this period, the accounts written by early Europeans in the area give us a glimpse into the history of Florida's melting pot cuisine.

Present-day Saint Augustine, Pensacola and Tampa were some of the first areas in which Spanish expeditions landed, followed by French exploration and the British invasion. Wheat, sugar, rice and bananas would soon be common foods from the East, and the West introduced maize to European countries. It started with Juan Ponce de León, who not only named the state but also, on his second voyage, sailed along the eastern coast past Cape Canaveral and the Dry Tortugas, making landfall somewhere along the central Gulf Coast, bringing with him seven Andalusia cows and laying the foundation for the cattle industry. Today, the cattle industry remains a strong part of the Florida economy.

Spanish explorers Pánfilo de Narváez and Hernando de Soto anchored their ships and came ashore in the Tampa Bay region. In 1528, Narvaez,

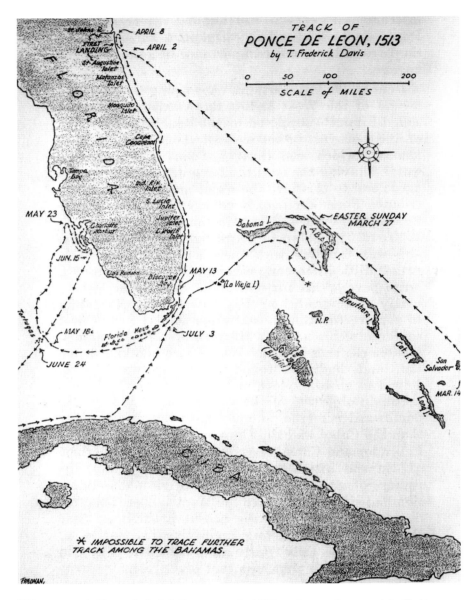

This map tracks Ponce de León's first voyage, in 1513, to the area he named *La Florida*.

landed on the west coast of Tampa Bay, bringing with him hundreds of men and many horses. He discovered a Tocobaga village near present-day Safety Harbor at the north end of Tampa Bay but continued northward, looking for a friendlier environment, as well as food and water. By the time he reached Saint Marks, in the northern part of the state, his plans to explore the area had changed. He and the other few survivors concentrated on getting out of the state. Some of the horses he brought were eaten, and the rest were lost along the way. These might have been the first horses in Florida since the ice age and were possibly the ancestors of the ones used by cowmen in the state's the cattle industry. Spanish settlers eventually turned Florida into America's first cattle-raising state. In addition to starting the cattle industry, the roots of the citrus industry were planted. The Spanish Crown ordered all ships bound for the West to carry cargoes of plants, seed and domesticated animals, thus planting the seeds for future generations to enjoy the bounty of citrus in Florida.

In 1539, Hernando de Soto landed somewhere along Tampa Bay, bringing with him priests, women, horses, mules, war dogs and pigs.

In 1539, Hernando de Soto, along with several hundred men, brought a herd of swine, today known as piney woods rooters or razorback hogs, and introduced the first pigs to Florida. The hog had no natural enemy and therefore reproduced easily and became a popular food choice for many. De Soto landed somewhere along Tampa Bay, and before he began his trek across the state, he rescued a young man left by Narváez, Juan Ortiz. Legends surround his name, as the basis for the familiar Pocahontas story, since an Indian princess at Pinellas Point in Saint Petersburg also saved Oritz.

De Soto marched inland, into the territory of the Timucua and Apalachee, through present-day Dade City. Along the way, the group ran out of potable water, and several people died in Zephyrhills as a result. Ironically, today the city is known for its fresh spring water. Traveling on through Ocala, Lake City and Live Oak, when they reached the Tallahassee area they marveled at the lush agriculture and decided to camp for several months, until winter was over, before leaving the state. The first Christmas in Florida, and possibly North America, might have been at this campsite in the Apalachee Indian village, in present-day Tallahassee. The Indians in the area deserted the town when De Soto arrived with his men, leaving behind their stored food.

In 1559, Don Tristán de Luna y Arellano of Spain, along with 1,500 soldiers and settlers, tried for two years to set up Florida's first settlement but failed. Their temporary settlement was called Santa Maria Bay, near present-day Pensacola Bay. After only one month, a hurricane ruined the supply of food they had stored on their ships. They lacked not only supplies but also the ability to produce food or grow their own and were dependent on the Indians to give them food, living mostly on shipboard supplies such as biscuits, hardtack, salted meat and fish, dried beans and peas along with wine, beer and cider. Hardtack was mass-produced by bake-houses of the Royal Navy. This dried biscuit stayed mold-free for up to a year. Sailors used the hardtack to create a breakfast soup of flour, water and lard. Later in the day, hardtack was eaten with wine stored in olive jars. Today, Luna's shipwreck artifacts are on display at the T.T. Wentworth Junior Museum in downtown Pensacola. The French influence is still felt in northwest Florida with the popularity of Cajun and Creole foods in the area.

The French, interested in colonizing, sent Jean Ribault, then René Goulaine de Laudonniére, along with sketch artist Jacques le Moyne to the Saint Augustine area. Moyne made the first drawings of the Timucua cooking their meat and fish on a barbacoa. One such drawing depicts a lattice-type grill over a smoky fire, probably of burning mangrove or buttonwood, which is dense and burns slowly. Unfortunately, almost all of these drawings were burned when the Spanish attacked and burned Fort Caroline. Later, le Moyne redrew the pictures from memory, but the accuracy of some of the details is questionable, such as the ears on the alligator. Theodor de Bry published a book of engravings he made of the drawings. The drawings and descriptions are still used today to study the life of the Timucua.

The French explorers and colonists were largely dependent on the Timucua for most provisions and supplies, except for cattle, pigs and poultry. Jean Ribault possibly introduced the first watermelon to the state, before he challenged Spanish claim to Florida, when he landed near Jacksonville at the mouth of the Saint Johns River and renamed it the River of May. The Spanish also carried watermelons with them from Africa to Europe before bringing them to the southern Native Americans. Ribault built a monument to signify France's claim on Florida. Two years later, Laudonniére founded Fort Caroline, a triangular wooden structure, at that location. Captain Laudonniére called a feast on June 30, 1564, and everyone sang a song of thanksgiving.

One of the most notable explorers and colonists was Pedro Menéndez de Avilés, who, in 1565, was ordered by Spain's king to destroy the French Huguenot colony. When he took over the fort, his troops acquired large quantities of flour, barrels of biscuits, bushels of wheat, a flour mill and some hogs. Menéndez founded Saint Augustine and named it in honor of the saint whose feast day it was when he first sighted land. This happened forty-two years before Jamestown was settled in 1607 and over fifty years before the Plymouth landing in 1620, making it the oldest European settlement in America. Menéndez is responsible for the first permanent settlement of Saint Augustine and, possibly, the first Thanksgiving dinner with the Timucua. The Sunshine State's first Thanksgiving dish might have been a Spanish stew with pork, garbanzo beans, sausage, fresh local vegetables, garlic and olive oil. Timucuans likely contributed local game and fish such as mullet, catfish, tortoise, oysters or clams. Eminent Florida historian Michael V. Gannon wrote, in his book *The Cross in the Sand*, "the feast day observed…after Mass, the Adelantado (Spanish governor to the area) had the Indians fed and dined himself. It was the first community act of religion and thanksgiving in the first permanent settlement in the land."

The Spanish built forts in the area to protect their interests against the English, French and Indians. To supplement the cattle, pigs and poultry, the Spanish planted corn, wheat, oats, pumpkins, garbanzo and other beans, as well as sugarcane. A *situado*, or annual allowance of cash, food

Pedro Menéndez founded Saint Augustine in 1565 and named it in honor of the saint whose feast day it was when he first sighted land.

and supplies, was sent to each Spaniard. They were not agriculturists, but in order to survive they adopted the diet and food-preparation techniques of the Timucua and soon were dining on cornbread and fish.

Research, done by C. Margaret Scarry and Elizabeth J. Reitz, on the subsistence of these early settlers shows a reliance on pig, deer, cows, sharks, sea catfish, drums and mullet. To supplement their protein sources, the Europeans replaced their common homeland staples of wheat, oats, rye and barley with corn, beans and squash. Growing wild in the area were nuts, berries, persimmons and grapes, along with edible weeds such as pigweed (also known as amaranth) and greenbrier. Other foods found were peas, figs, peaches and watermelons. Probably imported at first, they used lima beans, chili peppers, chickens and a variety of turtles common in the region. Raccoons, wild turkeys and other fowl, as well as seafood, were also found in the area.

With the abundance of seafood and plentiful game in the forests, along with rich soil for gardening and wild-growing fruits and vegetables, the variety of food available at the time of European contact was extraordinary. A radical shift in cooking took place with the introduction of French and Spanish influences. Improved nutritional sources and cooking methods were, in part, a result of the new foods and cooking styles that arrived from across the globe. Beef and dairy products, pork, chicken, citrus, wheat, oats, garbanzo beans, sugarcane, peaches, figs and other fruits were new to the Indians. Wine, olive oil and garlic were imported. Black-eyed peas, eggplant, collard greens and okra added variety to their once-limited vegetable choice. From Central and South America came sweet peppers and hot peppers, peanuts, tomatoes, chocolate and white potatoes.

A new age of dining and cooking in Florida had arrived with imported iron pots, knives, pottery and china. The Spanish used several types of ceramics for cooking, storage and eating. Lead-glazed earthenware was very common, and today *majolica*, tin-enameled earthenware, is valued for its beauty. Forks were not as common, so spoons or fingers were used. Some had personal knives with forked tips (perhaps the precursor to the spork of today's school lunches). Open-hearth cooking was introduced, leading to more baking. Across the state of Florida, the Spanish and French influences can still be found today, with delicious gumbos, soups and stews such as *caldo gallego* (a Spanish white bean and greens soup) and other foods that hold a key to the past, both in preparation style and ingredients used. This hearty fare must have been a welcome treat for those just arriving by ship from across the ocean.

Spanish missions thrived in Florida long before colonists arrived in Jamestown. The first multicultural communities in Florida go back to the establishment of missions across the state, where Native Americans and Spanish worked together to create more agricultural growth than ever before. The supply routes across the area became known as the Camino Real, which connected Saint Augustine to the Tallahassee area. With more than thirty successful missions from the Saint Augustine area inland across the state, the success rate was not as high in the southern part of the state with the Ais, Tequesta and Calusa. The Apalachee and Timucua were more settled and more receptive to the changes of lifestyle. They had been swapping goods for centuries with other natives. The Native Americans were taught new farming techniques and animal husbandry, such as how to raise chickens, cattle and hogs and how to grow grain and fruits. The Apalachee province served as headquarters for many of the Spanish missions in the area. Gannon writes of Bishop Calderon's experiences in Florida at a mission in the 1670s: "The ordinary diet of the Indians consisted of 'corn with ashes'—lye hominy—pumpkins, beans and such game and fish as they could catch. The usual beverage was water, and they never touched wine or rum." Today, at the living history museum of the Mission San Luis in Tallahassee, visitors can experience what it might have been like at a thriving mission in the early 1600s with "roosters crowing, dogs barking and stew cooking."

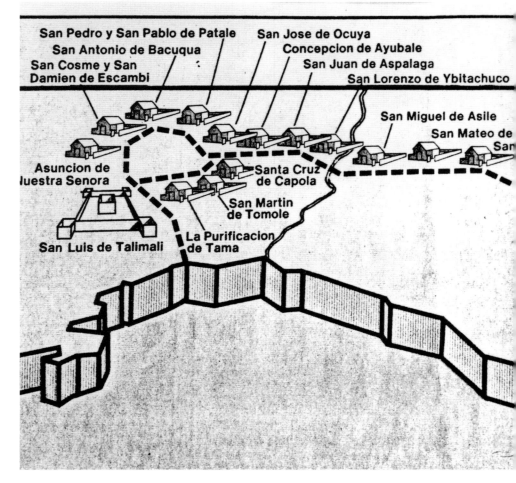

This map shows locations of missions from around 1630 across North Florida, from Saint Augustine to Mission San Luis, now an Apalachee-Spanish Living History Museum.

Many native Indians worked on farms or Spanish-owned ranches, known as *haciendas*, utilizing the kitchens and ovens, while others lived in villages near the mission. At the missions, some Indians were servants, cooking meals for the friars in a separate kitchen, also called a *cocina*. Others cleared fields and grew crops to feed themselves, the missionaries and the Spanish settlers in Saint Augustine. Cattle were kept nearby, and gardens were planted in the fertile soil to supply herbs, vegetables and fruits for food and medicinal and religious purposes. Some Indians still hunted buffalo; gathered wild foods

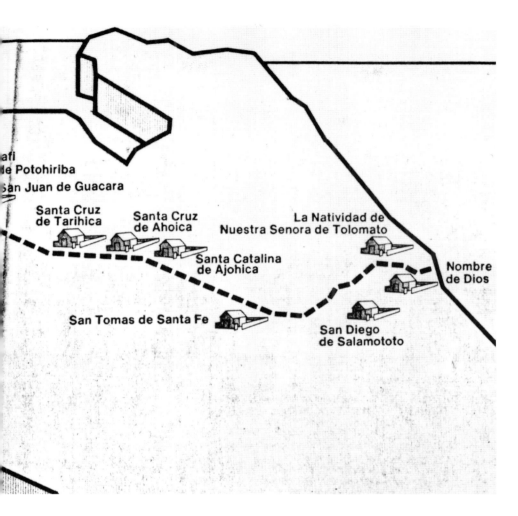

such as persimmons, berries, acorns and hickory nuts; collected turtles; and fished with spears and weirs. Dishes made with both the indigenous ingredients and those introduced by the Spanish produced a multicultural culinary combination. Native Americans were accustomed to using corn instead of wheat; venison, rabbit and water fowl instead of beef, pork or chicken; and ground nuts or bear fat instead of butter.

The Native Americans introduced a special ceremonial tea to the Spaniards, called black tea, or *cassina*. Made from the evergreen yaupon holly, one of the few caffeine-containing plants in Florida, its botanical name is *Ilex vomitoria*, which is a reflection of how some felt after drinking it. The plant leaves are prepared by drying and roasting them to make the caffeine more soluble. Then, they are boiled until frothy and strained. The resulting dark, reddish-brown tea was stimulating but, if not prepared properly, could be fatal. Jonathan Dickinson described the ritual surrounding cassina when he was shipwrecked among the Ais: "An Indian man, having a pot on the fire wherein he was making a drink of the leaves of a shrub (which we understood afterwards by the Spaniard, is called casseena), boiling said leaves, after they had parched them in a pot…the drink was made, and cooled to sup, was in a conch-shell…passed to the rest of the Casseekey's associates …but no other man woman or child." At the Spanish missions, this tea was served only in the council house unless the chief granted special permission to serve it elsewhere. Many native tribes throughout the state drank this special tea. Other drinks were made from leaves, bark or roots of plants and trees. Pine needle tea was another version, but a more enjoyable tea was made from the root of the sassafras tree.

At the missions, an elevated *garita*, or storage shed, was used to store the year's harvest of wheat and corn, along with fruits, berries, nuts and acorns. Venison, beef and fish were smoked and dried. Olive jars were used as storage vessels for water, wine and olive oil. Olive oil was used to protect cheeses and sausages. Later, wine was used to protect and pickle fruits and vegetables.

According to Milanich, "barley, cabbage, chickens, cucumbers, figs, garbanzo beans, garlic, European grapes and greens, hazelnuts, various herbs, lettuce, melons, oranges, peas, peaches, pigs, pomegranates, sugarcane, sweet potatoes, wheat and watermelons" have all been identified at mission sites. Other imported food items included Spanish onion, olives, honey, biscuits and cakes, along with foods they could not procure locally. Pottery made by the native women was beginning to resemble Spanish tableware with plates, pitchers and other dishware.

For the Spanish, the focus changed from the wheat, barley and rye of their homelands to maize, squash, beans and pumpkins. Eventually, wheat was imported and successfully grown on Spanish ranches and ground into flour to make bread. Egg custards and spices, along with the concept of three meals a day, were being introduced into the vast wilderness of *La Florida*. While the missions were being established, to the north, the first colonists in Jamestown brought with them horses, chicken, cattle, pigs, goats, sheep, ducks, geese, wheat, rye, barley, oats, apples, turnips, cabbage, wine, brandy, rum, malted brew, seeds and plants, including herbs and other food items such as hard cheese, bread, dried beans and salted meat for their journey at sea. "By the time the pilgrims came ashore at Plymouth, Saint Augustine was up for urban renewal," Gannon likes to point out. As Britain gained control over much of the land to the north, Spanish Florida began to fade.

During the seventeenth century, colonization in Florida consisted of a few scattered towns and small settlements along the coast, numerous outposts, cattle ranches and fishing ranchos. Just as the seeds of the citrus industry were already germinating, the Spanish also started the fishing industry in Florida. In the 1630s, Spanish fishermen from Cuba began to fish cooperatively with native Floridians. Small fishing settlements, called fishing ranchos, are documented from the Tampa Bay region to the southwest coast and the Florida Keys. By the 1780s, the Calusa were no longer a presence in the area, and their fishing sites were taken over by Cuban fishermen, some with Calusa refugees as guides. At first, Cuban fishermen set up seasonal fish camps, from August through March, but later established permanent ranchos.

Cattle ranching, an important part of the culture of the area, was spreading out across the central part of the state. Spanish-owned *haciendas* (cattle ranches and farms) were located in Timucua and Apalachee territory. Some of these ranches also produced wheat and corn. Using Native American labor, Rancho de La Chua, near Gainesville, was a major producer of cattle and pigs in the 1600s. The site of Hacienda de La Chua, located on the north rim of today's Paynes Prairie, is believed to have been the largest cattle ranch in Spanish Florida, operating until the early 1700s.

Cattle and wild horses seen on the prairie today are descendants of those brought over by the Spanish. Additional Spanish cattle ranches were scattered around Tallahassee, Gainesville, Palatka and Saint Augustine. The meat of the Florida cattle was tough and stringy, and Cuban dishes such as picadillo, using ground beef or the slow simmering ropa vieja, were popular choices to help soften the tough meat fibers. Cooking utensils were more advanced. Storage containers went from olive jars to wooden barrels and kegs. Woodenware was becoming more common, and ovens were being designed to accommodate the user. European explorers started a culinary exchange of foods and cooking supplies. They introduced even more utensils that made meal preparation less time-consuming and easier. Copper pots, porcelain, stoneware and pewter dishes were introduced. Glass bottles replaced clay containers, and silverware would soon become a regular part of the mealtime place setting.

Saint Augustine's rich culinary history was beginning to take shape as many Native American foods, preparation techniques and vessels for cooking and storage were embraced. Detached kitchens were added to households with a limited supply of kettles, skimmers, spits, pots and hooks, along with dishes for setting the table. Foods from Central and South America such as

In 1598, the public market on Saint Augustine's central plaza provided a storefront for residents to offer goods for sale to the general public. The structure was rebuilt in the 1800s.

sweet peppers, hot peppers, peanuts, tomatoes, lima beans, chocolate and white potatoes were becoming common ingredients. Hunting and fishing became last resorts because the Spanish settlers lacked the necessary skills and the desire to learn more about the art of hunting and fishing.

In 1598, a gristmill and the first public market in what became the United States was established in Saint Augustine. A standard system of measures and weights, used to protect the consumer, was also created. In *The King's Coffer*, Amy Bushnell describes the scene at the time: "Indians paddling canoes or carrying baskets brought their produce to the market on the plaza: twists of tobacco, pelts, painted wooden trays, packages of dried cassina tea leaves, rope and fishnets, earthenware and baskets, dried turkey meat, lard and salt pork, saddles and shoe leather, charcoal and fresh fish and game; especially they brought maize…Maize, not wheat, was the staff of life in Florida." The Spanish also enjoyed their imported olive oil, wheat flour, wine, sugar and chocolate.

New dishes were added to early Floridians' repertoires of recipes. Using heated stones in earth ovens for bread baking, the potages that extended over a fire or meat roasted on a spit, the creative cook could come up with hundreds of different taste combinations. Soups and stews were popular since they were easy to prepare and incorporated a wide variety of available ingredients.

4
Florida's First Chronicles of Travel

Arriving in Saint Augustine half-starved, with his infant son, wife and some of his shipmates, Jonathan Dickinson chronicled his 1696 story of shipwreck and survival as he traveled up the southeast coast of Florida. *Jonathan Dickinson's Journal* gives detailed descriptions of dining experiences that go from near starvation in the southern part of Florida to a bountiful feast when he finally reached Saint Augustine on his way to Philadelphia. The group encountered friendly Indians who not only shared their food, but nursed the infant as well. Other times, they were reduced to eating the scraps of rotten food left by some of the more hostile tribes.

Freshly caught fish was served raw or cooked. "Our Indian brought a fish boiled on a small palmetto leaf," noted Dickinson. He was impressed with the skill of the Indian chief's son when he saw him "with his striking staff to the inlet to strike fish for us; which he performed with great dexterity…sometimes running swiftly…and seldom missed when he darted at them. In two hours' time he got as many fish as would serve twenty men." At times, the group dined on oysters and an abundance of fish. Dickinson describes the preparation of cassina from yaupon holly leaves, and fish "boiled with scales, head and gills, and nothing taken from them but the guts." Palmetto berries, used for medicinal purposes today, were described as, "rotten cheese steeped in tobacco." Several times, being offered the berries, they turned them down as "the taste was so irksome and ready to take our breath from us." Dickinson noticed, "These people neither sow nor plant any manner of thing whatsoever, nor care for anything but what the barren sand produces;

fish they have as plenty as they please," along with cocoplums and sea grapes, when in season. Spaniards whom Dickinson's group later encountered shared some of their scant provisions, and the group was lucky enough to later find pumpkin vines with tiny pumpkins, many of which they roasted right away, while saving others to be boiled later.

When Dickinson and his family arrived in Saint Augustine, they were offered wine and hot chocolate. Spanish explorers introduced hot chocolate to society around 1519, after they observed the Aztecs drinking it, and by 1544, it was being imported to Europe. Valued at first for medical purposes, it is fitting that the governor of Saint Augustine should offer it to the weary and half-starved travelers when they arrived in his town. (By 1753, the Industrial Revolution and mass production made chocolate available for the general population.) After a few weeks, the Dickinson group moved on to the north, leaving the large orchards of oranges, lemons, limes, figs and peaches growing there, along with Indian corn, peas and herbs.

By the early 1700s, British colonists and the Creeks from Georgia and Alabama were pushing south and eventually came into North Florida. After

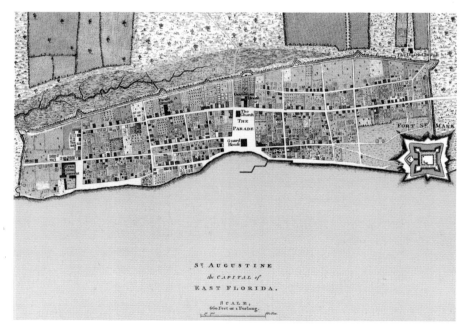

During the British period from 1763 to 1783, Florida was divided into two parts. The capital of West Florida was Pensacola. The capital of East Florida, as shown in this map, was Saint Augustine.

the destruction of the Spanish missions by the British and the Creeks, a battle waged for control of North Florida. The French and Indian War, in 1750, and the American Revolution, in 1776, brought about many changes as Florida was becoming home to an influx of new people.

Jerald T. Milanich wrote, "Scholars agree the name Seminole was originally derived from the Spanish word cimarrone," meaning Indians living apart from missions. Others credit the British with naming the Creek "Seminoles." The Creek, Miccosukee and Seminole are often collectively called Seminoles since many Creek became Seminoles. The Creek, Miccosukee and escaped slaves filled the void left by all other indigenous tribes who were either forced out or died as a result of war and disease.

Saint Augustine was not the only town to experience an influx of different nationalities. To the west, Pensacola—also know as "The City of Five Flags" because it has been ruled under the Spanish, French, British, Confederate and American flags—changed hands several times between the Spanish and French. However, the British period (1763–83) in Florida was a more peaceful and prosperous time when the state was divided into two regions. The capital of East Florida was Saint Augustine, and the capital of West Florida was Pensacola, with the Apalachicola River as the dividing line. At that time, West Florida also included a portion of Louisiana. The English promoted settlements and exploration of the interior as they developed the surrounding natural resources. Roads were laid out, and for a while, the new settlers were at peace with the American Indians.

Today, Historic Pensacola Village features houses from the late 1770s to the early 1800s, showing how these early settlers lived and prepared their meals. The largest single ethnic group at the time was the French Creole. These free descendants of Spanish citizens with African ancestry were developing a cooking style all their own. The people of this multicultural town were using Chinese teacups and German stoneware, Mexican pottery and Majolica earthenware, and were enjoying both imported and indigenous foods. South America, Africa and Europe all contributed to their global diet and Creole heritage.

Many of the new settlers arriving in Florida were accustomed to the luxuries of colonial life, with an open hearth and fireplace or an outdoor wood-fired brick oven. A movable crane to support large pots and pans over a fire replaced the old-fashioned "lug" pole. Suspended from the side of the fireplace, the crane could be swung around for heat control or for serving. Chimneys served as smokehouses, and potatoes and eggs were roasted among the ashes. Andirons with spits used for roasting meat were becoming more common. Pots and kettles with legs, known by some as "spiders," and long-legged iron trivets for holding pots and pans above the coals were placed among the fiery hot ashes and coals.

Other common cooking items included dripping pans and Dutch ovens with concave lids on which hot coals were placed for cooking. Many cooks also had other basic equipment such as knives and cleavers, meat forks and spoons. A well-equipped kitchen would have had a colander, strainer, sieve, mortar and pestle, sugar nipper, rolling pin and extra baking tins or molds. Waffles were made using a hand-held waffle iron, which was suspended over the fire.

Boards hung from the kitchen ceiling, attached by ropes, were used as cupboards. The kitchen itself was a multi-purpose room, used for preparing food and eating during the day and for sleeping at night. There was no public market in Pensacola at the time, but the food supply included beef, seafood and vegetables grown in private gardens. Soups and stews for dinner were cooked inside at the hearth or outside in the summer in order to keep the house cool. Tomatoes and potatoes became staples in soup making after they were introduced to the area. The British expanded their agricultural presence from home gardens to plantation-style farming. In 1868, a book was published based on the George R. Fairbanks lectures of the history of Florida, *The Spaniards in Florida*. He describes the Saint Augustine home: "gardens were well stocked with fruit trees,...figs, guavas, plantain, pomegranates, lemons, limes, citrons, shaddock, bergamot...oranges,...pot-herbs...were seldom destroyed by cold."

By 1764, the last of the indigenous Florida Indians were sent to Cuba with the Spanish. With the British in control, the Plantation Period in Florida began. The English government offered land grants to wealthy Englishmen for the establishment of plantations. One of the larger plantations at New Smyrna left a particular legacy of multicultural cooking. In 1768, Dr. Andrew Turnbull, a British colonizer, brought over one thousand indentured laborers from the Mediterranean, including the island of Minorca, to an area just south of Saint Augustine, called New Smyrna, to work his indigo plantation. At the plantation, their small kitchen gardens included common crops such as watermelons, cucumbers, corn, peas, beans, potatoes, peppers, onions and greens. Although olive trees grew in the area, they were not sufficient enough to produce olive oil, a common ingredient in the Mediterranean laborers' homeland. Fish, shellfish and gopher tortoise were plentiful, though (if they had time to catch them), with the most familiar fish being mullet. Lisa is the Spanish name for mullet, which is pleasant-sounding but never caught on

Plantation ruins along the Indian River from one of Turnbull's warehouses, built of coquina in 1768.

as the official name of this popular fish. Today, the common mullet is also being harvested for its roe, considered a delicacy in some places. Here in Florida, the roe is often rolled in cornmeal and fried.

By 1777, the Turnbull plantation had failed, but the six hundred survivors, the majority being Minorcans with some Greeks and Italians as well, walked seventy miles to Saint Augustine, where many settled on Charlotte Street. The failed Minorcan colony has had a lasting influence on Saint Augustine cooking with the introduction of the Datil pepper used to flavor stews, sauces, pilaus and other dishes. "Mullet on the Beach" was commonly shouted out as the fishermen announced their catch. Many were already familiar with fish and shrimp from their homeland. Others were farmers and brought those skills with them. The Saint Augustine area provided some of the staples of their native diets, like lemon and eggplant, which could easily be grown there. Sea turtles and their eggs were another common food for them. Kitchens were small, so cooking was usually done in open pots and braziers, which could be moved outdoors as the weather allowed. A large bread oven of mortared coquina was recently excavated from the central part of the New

Smyrna town site, as well as a small bread oven next to a farmhouse. These types of ovens are still in use today in Minorca and other parts of the world. Breakfast might be a simple combination of bread, olive oil, vinegar, salt and pepper called bread salad. By then, the King's Bakery had been built to supply bread for the troops. Then back under Spanish control, Bernardo Segui, of Minorcan descent, was a baker to the garrison, living in what is known today as the historic Segui-Kirby Smith House. To supplement meals, bread was served with a dish of vinegar, olive oil, grated radishes and minced onion, or toasted bread was served with a little chopped tomato, garlic, basil, vinegar, olive oil and lemon juice—similar to today's Italian bruschetta.

Kitchen gardens and small orchards surrounded homes and other areas near town. The main meal, usually eaten in the middle of the day, was often a stew of onion, garlic and peppers to which meat or fish were added. Peppers were the main ingredient in their vegetable stews, called *sopas*. Datil peppers are a part of the Minorcan legacy influencing cookery in Saint Augustine. These slender, yellow-green, homegrown peppers are still being used in the area and are synonymous with Minorcan cooking. The Minorca-style pilau was a common dish, usually composed of rice cooked with Datil peppers and a protein source, such as pork, shellfish and/or chicken. A special version, called gopher stew, consisted of land turtle enhanced with bacon, onion, garlic, tomatoes, potatoes, thyme, Datil pepper, flour, salt and pepper. Many variations of this popular dish later became a Cracker specialty of the Florida backwoods, also known as perloo (also spelled purloo). Minorcan Datil chowder is being prepared today, with contests and cook-offs still searching for the best, all using the hot Datil pepper. Most commonly found in the Saint Augustine area, it resembles the habenero but has a more intense sweet citrus flavor. Today, this rare pepper is hard to find outside of the Saint Augustine area. George R. Fairbanks describes the Saturday night before Easter, when young men would stroll from house to house, serenading neighbors and hoping for a gift of food such as *fromajardis*, a traditional Easter pastry seasoned with nutmeg and stuffed with cheese. It's then baked until the cheese melts, oozing out of the cross cut on the top. Minorcan crispees were made from the leftover dough, sprinkled with cinnamon sugar and baked until golden brown.

A *Revolution in Eating* was about to occur, as James E. McWilliams describes in his book. The English colonists were trying to establish cotton plantations in Florida and brought with them their southern and plantation cooking styles. They found the wild orange trees established by the Spanish, who brought citrus seeds that eventually grew into groves across the state. With orange and other citrus trees being cultivated, along with cotton, rice, sugarcane and indigo, productive plantations were established. Three meals a day were becoming the norm, especially on plantation-style farms. New foods were introduced, such as cucumbers and honey. The razorback hog was growing wild as herds ran through the center of town. (Later, sport hunters introduced the true European wild boar into certain parts of the country, and they have mixed with these wild swine.) Dinner, a large meal served at midday, included meat, fish, poultry, side dishes, seasonal fruit, vegetables, bread, butter and sometimes jam. At night, just before bedtime, a light snack of fruit, nuts or cheese was often enjoyed.

William Bartram, a thirty-five-year-old Quaker naturalist, explored the Florida wilderness and recalled some of his experiences in a book, published in 1791, called *Travels and Other Writings*. Bartram describes the Suwannee River and his encounters with Florida Seminoles and Creeks who invited him to dine with them. At that time, the Alachua Seminoles were raising cattle and horses.

Bartram wrote of wild orange groves and alligators, along with various and abundant fish. Returning to his camp one night, he recalled a dinner of broiled fish and rice "and having with me oil, pepper and salt and excellent oranges hanging in abundance over my head (a valuable substitute for vinegar)." He describes the bays and lagoons being full of "oysters, and varieties of other shell-fish, crabs, shrimp…The clams, in particular, are large, their meat white, tender and delicate." He also mentioned the excellent fish found along the coast, sounds and inlets such as "rock, bass, drum, mullet, sheepshead, whiting, gouper, flounder, sea trout, (this last seems to be a species of cod) skate, skipjack, stingray." He described one way fish was prepared for eating: "cover them whole in hot embers, where they bake them; the skin with the scales easily peels, leaving the meat white and tender." He spoke of mudfish tasting like mud and the delicious-tasting soft-shell tortoises, marveling at the abundance of dining options with the herds of deer, flocks of turkey and myriads of fish.

While Bartram was visiting the Seminole village of Cuscowilla at Paynes Town, now known as Paynes Prairie, Chief Cowkeeper served "venison, stewed with bear's oil, fresh corn cakes, milk and hominy; and our drink, honey and water, very cool and agreeable." Later, after exploring the prairie and upon arrival at the council house, a banquet of barbecued ribs, bowls and kettles of stewed fish, broth and "tripe soup; it is made from the belly or paunch of the beef, not overcleansed of its contents, cut and minced pretty fine, and then made into a thick soup, seasoned well with salt and

William Bartram spoke of mudfish tasting like mud, but he enjoyed dining on the delicious-tasting soft-shell tortoises as featured in this drawing of his.

aromatic herbs; but the seasoning not quite strong enough to extinguish its original savour and scent."

According to Bartram, the Creek never ate nor planted irish potatoes, but some of the other foods mentioned were spanish potatoes, squash, pumpkins, watermelons, peaches, oranges, plums, grapes, figs and some apples. They also used both the fruit and roots of a vast array of wild or native vegetables. One example, a species of smilax, with a multi-step process to prepare, yields a delicious and nutritious product from the tuberous sprouts. They must be dug up, chopped, macerated, soaked, drained and dried and then mixed with boiling water, which yielded a jelly that is sweetened with honey or sugar or mixed with corn flour and fried in bear's grease for a corn cake or fritter.

When Bartram visited what is known today as the oldest house in Saint Augustine, the Gonzales-Alverez House, most kitchens were outfitted with copper pots, knives, forks, wooden spoons and stirrers. If you were wealthy, there were also silver bowls and utensils along with ornate pottery, porcelain from the Orient, chocolate cups from England and bone-handled utensils. The commoners ate from pewter, tin or wood and drank from pewter mugs and black-lead glazed cups, also using pewter forks and knives. Containers for storage ranged from hand-blown glass bottles to

When Bartram visited what today is known as the oldest house in Saint Augustine, on Saint Francis Street, most kitchens were outfitted with copper pots, knives, forks and spoons.

baskets, barrels, boxes, casks and canvas bags. During the Second Spanish period, in 1783–1821, detached kitchens were used to keep the heat and fire away from the main house. This trend continued until the advent of air conditioning.

5
The First Seminoles

The Seminoles were descendants of various Creek tribes who moved into Florida before Andrew Jackson claimed it as a territory. The Seminole Wars began before the Civil War and continued past it. After war "too complex in its operations and too varied in its vicissitudes to be dealt with in detail here," as George M. Barbour so eloquently put it in his 1882 book, *Florida for Tourists, Invalids, and Settlers*, Native Americans were forced to go west. Some stayed in North Florida, while others, in order to elude capture, found their way to the Florida Everglades. Alongside escaped slaves, they made lives for themselves in the swampland of South Florida as the rest of the state was being settled with plantations and pioneers.

Just as the Seminole filled the void left by the aboriginals, scrub cattle filled the void left by the bison that once roamed the area. The scrub cattle continued to thrive in Florida, as did citrus. After the Third Seminole War ended in 1858, the cattle industry emerged, and the Seminole Indians created a way of life around gardens and herds of horses and cattle. Later, a symbiotic relationship developed between them and the Florida Crackers. The Seminole also befriended and helped out many plantation owners, sometimes bringing venison, honey, bear meat and buffalo tongue, as chronicled by Denys Rolle in *Humble Petition*.

Before old trading posts became gambling casinos and the reservations of the Miccosukee and the Seminole became home to lavish resorts, large citrus groves and cattle ranches, the Seminole were forced to find new methods for survival. Following the traditions of their ancestors, and learning to live off the land, they continued to show gratitude to their creator for providing food with the annual "Green Corn Dance," which marked the start of a new cycle for the year. They started by drinking *cassina*, also called the "black drink," of their ancestors, followed by fasting and then the beginning of the festival.

Bernard Romans, in *A Concise Natural History of East and West Florida*, describes his experience in the late 1700s of the Native American approach to food preparation: "Their common food is the zea or the Indian corn, of which they make meal, and boil it; they also parch it, and then pound it; thus taking it on their journey, they mix it with cold water, and will travel a great way without any other food...they likewise use hickory nuts in plenty, and make a milkey liquor of them, which they call milk of nuts...and eat it with sweet potatoes in it." Seminoles continued to use the highly nutritious acorn for food, flour and oil. Leaching out the tannins in acorns is another skill the Native Americans perfected, and they used the nuts in various dishes, including bread, soups and stews. Another treat was to cut a hole in an orange, pour honey in it and then roast it over a fire.

They lived a lifestyle similar to the earlier Spanish missions in some ways, as communal living was necessary for survival. According to Clay MacCauley, in his report to the Bureau of Ethnology in the late 1800s, "A good sized kettle, containing stewed meat and vegetables, is the center around which the family gathers for its meal. This, placed in some convenient spot on the ground near the fire, is surrounded by more or fewer members of the household in a sitting posture." Hunting, fishing, farming and raising livestock provided ample food sources for the Seminole of the Florida everglades. Fish were speared or shot with bows and arrows, mostly by the children, while the men relied on the hook-and-line method for fishing and the rifle for hunting, after stalking their game on foot. The Florida everglades provided them with an abundance of wildlife such as deer, opossums, rabbits, squirrels, bears, terrapins, frogs, ducks, quails and turkeys. From the waterways, turtles and oysters were consumed. As MacCauley noted, "fifty cattle...and that the Seminole probably possess a thousand swine and five hundred chicken." To supplement wild fruits, their gardens provided them with pumpkins, melons, squash, sweet potatoes, beans, peas, corn and potatoes. Cornmeal, syrup, cane juice and bananas were common food choices, as the fertile soil produced these crops in abundance. MacCauley explains that to make cornmeal, "the corn is hulled and the germ cut out, so that there is only a pure white residue. This is then reduced by mortar and pestle to an almost impalpable dust. From this flour a cake is made, which, is said to be very pleasant to the taste."

Photographed by world-renowned photographer Joseph Janney Steinmetz in 1951, this Seminole woman standing in a dugout canoe with her children might be gigging for fish or frogs.

Sugarcane provides "sirup" and cane juice. MacCauley felt it "deserving to mention that the Seminole have around their houses at least a thousand banana plants." Cypress log canoes were used for traveling through swamps to reach trading posts to swap hides, racoon and deer for salt pork, wheat flour, coffee and salt.

Seminole Susie Billie, with her children Bob and Martha in the Florida Everglades, cooking over an open wood fire in the 1950s.

Anthropologist Alanson Skinner, working for the American Museum of Natural History in New York, observed the Seminole and noted: "Early in the morning one is usually awakened by the thump, thump, thump, of the women pounding corn, the squealing of pigs, and the crowing of roosters. After a heavy breakfast, the men take their rifles and depart, some to hunt, some to cultivate their cornfields, and others to spear turtles and fish…one of the houses of the village (usually the large one) is reserved for eating, and here food, generally sofki (sofkee—a ground corn dish), venison, biscuits or corn bread and coffee, is always ready for the hungry." Twice a day, in the morning and evening, the Seminole had regular meals, but eating between times was a common practice. Cooking turtles in their shells by roasting before the fire was a novel way of having fresh meat. Turtle shells have been found with holes drilled in them as the turtles would be tethered for easy keeping. MacCauley goes on to say, "The Seminole, however, though observing meal times with some regularity, eats just as his appetite invites. If it happens that he has a side of venison roasting before the fire he will cut from it at any time during the day and, with the piece of meat in one hand and a bit of Koonti or of different bread in the other, satisfy his appetite."

These Native Indians' resourcefulness in extracting foods from plants that appeared inedible, such as the coontie plant and sabal palm, was remarkable.

Some of the native plants growing in Florida eaten by the aboriginals are still grown and enjoyed today, either raw or cooked in recipes. One of the most notable early accomplishments, arguably South Florida's first industry, was the introduction of processing starch from the roots of the coontie plant (a species of *Zamia*, also known as comptie, koontie or Indian bread root), which became a staple of the South Floridian diet for both settlers and Seminoles. Laborious and time consuming, the process involved extracting starch from this ancient fernlike plant (used in landscaping and floral arrangements today). The roots, stems and leaves all contain a poisonous toxin if left raw, but the abundantly growing underground tuberous roots contain both the water-soluble toxin and the edible starch. After digging up the root, it was washed, chopped, pounded with a mortar and pestle, ground into a pulp and then mixed with water. Using a straining cloth, the starch was separated out into a container and would settle at the bottom while the water was drained off. A starchy paste was left to ferment before being spread on palmetto leaves to dry in the sun.

The knowledge necessary to maintain the technique was passed along to the Seminole from the former native tribes in the area, and they used the starch to make bread and pudding. Later settlers improved on the crude methods by using processing mills and increasing the number of fermentations, thereby producing a more refined product of pure white. MacCauley was at a factory in Miami where he was served coontie pudding with milk and guava jelly, which he found delicious. Commercial mills sold the starch to national baking companies for biscuits, crackers, cookies and spaghetti. Recipes are found in early cookbooks for puddings and jelly using various forms of the product. Northern biscuit makers called it Florida arrowroot starch.

Mary Randolph's *The Virginia Housewife* (1824), includes a recipe stating: "This pudding made of milk and arrow-root with six eggs, butter, sugar, nutmeg and a little grated lemon peel was to be baked and topped with sifted sugar and garnished with citron." An arrow-root jelly recipe that appeared in *The American Frugal Housewife* by Mrs. Child (1833) required a large spoonful of arrow-root powder mixed with boiling water, seasoned with nutmeg and sweetened with sugar, for the invalid. *The Florida Tropical Cook Book* (1912) includes a list of "Suggestions and Rules for Using Florida Arrowroot Starch." It was used in recipes for gravies, ice creams, fruit jellies and also as an addition to your laundry or an aide for burns.

The Seminole lived in *chickees*, derived from earlier dwellings of the Timucua and Calusa. These were open-sided, palm-thatched shelters, some

Seminole Indians created a cooking fire in a unique way by placing the logs in a spoke-like fashion, pushing them to the center as they burned.

elevated to avoid critters on the ground and others floorless to allow a fire to be built on the ground for cooking. Large logs, usually cypress, were arranged like spokes on a tire with the fire continually burning at the center. As the logs burned, they were pushed farther into the fire. If properly tended, the fire could last for weeks. A large pot would hang over the fire with an all-day snack of steaming sofkee, and the carved wooden sofkee spoon would be available for anyone in the village who wanted to eat.

Sofkee was a regular part of the Seminole diet and is still prepared in some Seminole households today. Made of corn meal and water, it was cooked until milky-looking and served hot from the pot. Sofkee has been described as a beverage-like porridge or corn soup. Sometimes, ashes from the fire were added to give flavor to the dish, depending on the type of wood being burned, with hickory being the most common used for this purpose. These ashes also helped to increase the nutritional value of the corn by helping to release the niacin and provide for a more balanced diet. The dried corn was pounded with a large cypress-wood mortar and pestle, so large it required standing to use it, until it was at the right consistency for sofkee. One hour of grinding might yield anywhere

Using a shared sofkee spoon, a pot of sofkee could be found hanging over the fire to eat anytime the Seminoles felt hungry. You can see the chickee in the background.

from one-half to four cups of cornmeal, depending on the strength of the grinder. Alanson Skinner explained how dried corn was pounded into meal with a mortar and pestle and then sifted and "winnowed by being tossed into the air, the breeze carrying away the chaff, while the heavier, edible portions of the corn falls back into the flat receiving basket." Kernels were placed in a kettle with sand and parched. Stirring with the sand helped keep the corn from burning. "When sufficiently parched, the corn is crushed in a mortar, and with the occasional addition of sugar, makes a delicious food. A little of the meal is sometimes added to water for use as a cooling drink," explains Mary Tiger from Ah-tah-thi-ki, the Seminole museum on the Big Cypress Reservation in South Florida. "We ate about three times a day, but when I was a child, I could eat when I got hungry. The food would be cooked and left on the table at the eating chickee. I would get sofkee and bread to eat. The food was placed in large plates with lids. We could get our food when we were hungry. The men went hunting early in the morning and stayed out until later in the day, so they ate two times a day."

Swamp cabbage, as described by F. Trench Townshend in the 1895 book *Wild Life in Florida: With a Visit to Cuba*, starts with a beautiful description of the sabal palm (also known as the cabbage palm or palmetto palm), the state tree of Florida:

On the shores of Lake Myakka I first tasted the "cabbage" of the cabbage-palm… in the south of the peninsula it is one of the most beautiful of trees. Rising straight [with a] and graceful trunk to a height varying from sixty to one hundred and twenty feet without a branch, it then bursts into a mass of dark-green fan-shaped leaves; in the center of this mass, protected by numerous fibrous folds, is the tender white shoot called the "cabbage," easily cut out with a hunting knife by one accustomed to the work, but difficult enough to the uninitiated. In taste it resembles a Spanish chestnut, and is eaten both raw and boiled.

Since state law now protects the tree, the Swamp Cabbage Festival in LaBelle is a great place to go for a taste of this Florida treat, named for its edible core, a crisp white cylinder eaten raw, pickled or boiled like cabbage. At one time, the Miccosukee harvested it for processing and canning. Much like hearts of palm found in the grocery store, the canned version can be used in place of fresh swamp cabbage but pales in comparison. Talking with Seminoles living in the Fort Myers area, they told me how they procure and prepare swamp cabbage: First, find a tree on private property and get permission to cut it down, since

Florida arrowroot starch or flour was made at this comptie (koontie) mill in Biscayne, Florida. John Kunkel Small photographed it in 1916.

Swamp cabbage can still be found at a few restaurants across the state, such as the Holopaw Restaurant in Central Florida, where it was featured as a special for the day. *Photographed by Joy Sheffield Harris.*

state law prohibits cutting unless on private property. Once the tree is cut, strip the outer boots (each frond makes layers or boots) from the trunk and fronds from the head, and then peel away the outer layers to reveal the tender heart. They even gave me some swamp cabbage tips: The longer the palm fronds, the more cabbage inside, and the smaller trees with long fronds are best. Cut one or two feet below where palm fronds emerge. For cooking, just add salt, pepper, pork and sugar to a pot of boiling water; put in the chopped cabbage; and simmer for thirty minutes or up to a few hours.

Sagamité is another corn dish of Native Americans. A recipe for Indian sagamité appears in the 1863 *Confederate Receipt Book,* calling for three parts Indian meal to one part brown sugar to be browned over the fire to appease hunger and thirst. Another method used by Native Americans included adding flour and wrapping the mixture in the corn leaves to be baked under the ashes and served with bear fat or honey. Roasted corn on the cob, easily prepared, was another way of cooking corn. By sticking a sharp stick through the cob, removing the silks and replacing the husks for protection, then rotating the corn over the flame until done, one can create a slow-roasted corn on the cob. This technique continued as a novelty way of cooking in the later years for tourists and travelers to Florida.

Today, the headquarters of the Florida Tribe of Eastern Creek Indians is located at Bruce, in northwest Florida, with a small museum and library belonging to the Florida Tribe of Eastern Creek Indians and the Choctawhatchee Clan of Creeks. To the south, reservations occupied by Seminole and Miccosukee exist in areas across South and Central Florida, with a Seminole Indian museum at the Big Cypress Reservation in South Florida. Technological advances eventually changed the way of life for Native Americans, but before their patchwork designs were created using sewing machines and before self-rising flour was added to their breads, they had an abundant and varied food supply provided by their environment.

While visiting the Florida Tribe of Eastern Creek in North Florida, I was furnished with recipes for Old-Time Apalachicola Creek Indian Stew, both the original recipe and the modern-day version. While the original recipe called for bear grease and venison or turtle meat, the modern version replaced them with vegetable oil and beef. The recipe for Indian Campfire Stew basically goes like this: Brown two pounds stew meat in oil, add chopped onion and stir. Add remaining vegetables (potatoes, corn and beans) and cook "until it starts smelling really good."

Fry bread is another Seminole food that is still prepared at festivals and cooking demonstrations. Watching the Seminole woman pinch off a ball of dough and drop it into the vat of boiling oil made me want to try it at home. Following her example, this is how to prepare fry bread at home: Heat enough oil to cover the fry bread in a large, deep, flat-bottomed pan until very hot. Take about two cups self-rising flour and mix with about two-thirds of a cup of water, using one hand to mix the flour while slowly adding water with the other hand. Then carefully place golf ball–sized balls of dough in the hot oil and cook about five seconds per side. Use a fork or slotted spoon to turn and brown the bread on both sides.

This Seminole Indian at the Brighton Reservation is preparing dough for fry bread, a treat still being made today for celebrations and special occasions. Photographed by Irvin M. Peithmann in the 1950s.

When done, place on a paper towel to drain. Serve hot, sprinkled with powdered sugar. When self-rising flour was introduced, the Seminoles of South Florida were quick to adopt it, making the preparation of bread even easier.

6
Cookbooks and the Sunshine State

As the Sunshine State was in the throes of becoming a United States territory, the Industrial Revolution made an impact on cooking and dining across the globe. A new capital city was established in Tallahassee in 1824, a year before Florida became the twenty-seventh state. The publication of literature, newspapers and cookbooks, with descriptive details of foods never before tasted, and other voices from the past shaped the culinary experience. Newspapers such as the *Florida Gazette*, the *Pensacola Gazette* and the *West Florida Advertiser* featured advertisements for cooking supplies and described a variety of foods and dishes from exotic countries.

With the written word more readily available, culinary experimentation was more easily shared. Home cooks were practicing chemistry through mixing and heating. Those taking notes and writing down the results would capture the essence of their time through recipes. Cookbooks tell a story about the culture and environment of the cooks and the people who ate the food. In the early 1800s, Jean Anthelme Brillat-Savarin wrote the culinary classic *The Physiology of Taste*, with such aphorisms as "Tell me what you eat, and I shall tell you what you are" and "The discovery of a new dish does more for human happiness than the discovery of a star."

British plantations concentrated in Middle Florida helped lay the foundation for southern cooking. New settlers brought new ideas and new ways of cooking, introducing such dishes as the English apple pie, Dutch cookies, coleslaw and German sauerkraut. New names were introduced:

This map of Florida in 1831 features fifteen counties and a Seminole reservation, along with insets of Pensacola and Tallahassee.

snickerdoodle, flummery, fool, crisp, crumble, cobbler, buckle, Betty, pandowdy, syllabub, slip, shrub, slump, grunt, salamander, rusk and jumble. American cookbooks were first published with traditional dishes reflecting their English heritage but later were adapted using indigenous ingredients such as pumpkin and corn. Cooking in the New England cities, with their servants, silver, white bread and imported cheeses, was vastly different from the wilderness territory that was Florida.

New recipes began to emerge just as foods, cooking styles and techniques were changing. The introduction of cookbooks, imported food and the uniform cooking of dishes was a prelude to restaurants. Before cookbooks were commonplace, however, new cooks watched mothers, sisters, aunts or other women preparing foods, using the same skills as their ancestors. In this way, cooking traditions were passed on from one generation to the next. Other than notes quickly jotted down, little time was available for creating and recording new recipes except in wealthier households. Women were busy cleaning, gardening, taking care of the pigs and poultry and milking cows. Few settlers in Florida could read or write, so manuscripts were rare, but oral traditions sustained many. Cooking was often common sense or, for the naturally talented gourmand, a gift from God.

An enlightening example of a handwritten manuscript is *Martha Washington's Booke of Cookery and Booke of Sweetmeats*. Passed down in 1749 from the mother of Martha Washington's first husband, Daniel Custis, she in turn passed it along to her granddaughter. The book stayed in the family until 1892 as new receipes were added along the way, and today finds a home at the Historical Society of Pennsylvania. Recipes were often called "receipts," and the term continued until right before World War II. But "recipe" was also used in the sixteenth century, as it is today. Two reproductions of the manuscript include: *The Martha Washington Cook Book*, in which Marie Kimball "modernized" or rewrote some recipes to 1940s standards, and *Martha Washington's Booke of Cookery*, transcribed by Karen Hess in 1981.

In the early 1800s, the great-grandniece of George Washington, Catherine Daingerfield Willis, married Napoleon Bonaparte's nephew, Prince Achille Murat. Prince Murat had moved from Saint Augustine, and the plantation Parthenope, to Tallahassee, and the plantation Lipona (east of Tallahassee). That is where he met Catherine and gained a reputation for hosting lavish dinner parties, serving dishes such as cows' ear stew, alligator steak and alligator tail soup, turkey buzzard stew (although he commented that the baked turkey buzzard wasn't so good) and roasted crow, along with boiled owl, lizards and rattlesnakes. Born in France, the prince came from a family of cooks, his father being the son of an innkeeper and waiter. After Prince Murat's death in 1847, Catherine purchased a plantation home, first worked by slaves and later by free blacks. The home, Bellevue, was moved from its original location to the Tallahassee Museum of History and Natural Science grounds. A reproduction of the detached kitchen is on display behind the house. The Murat House at Saint George and Bridge Street in Saint Augustine is now part of the Dow Museum of Historic Houses.

Florida had not yet become a state when Susannah Carter wrote and rewrote *The Frugal Housewife, or Complete Woman Cook*, including an appendix with American recipes. Her work on the book lasted from 1772 to 1803. Reay Tannahill, in the book *Food in History*, expressed the sentiment that "if English cooking was as bad as everyone except the English said it was, it was not for lack of cookery books," and these books had an enormous impact on cooking in America. Eleanor Lowenstein produced a bibliography of cookbooks, *American Cookery Books 1742 to 1860*, including different and numerous editions of several books. Not all together different, there are some changes from Carter's 1772 copy to the 1803 one, including drawings by Paul Revere demonstrating the best techniques for carving meats and an appendix with new recipes adapted to the foods and cooking styles in America. Carter's book had a profound impact on cookbooks written around that time. Hannah Glasse used the same appendix with similar recipes. Amelia Simmons used the same syllabub and other recipes. Lydia Marie Child did a remake by adding "American" to her book title, along with other changes. It was Mary Randolph who, in 1824, wrote one of the first grass-roots American cookbooks, *The Virginia Housewife*.

Even though printed recipes were available and making their way south from New England, with such treats as cakes, custards and ice cream, not all the cooks in Florida could read, limiting their culinary experimenting. An early cookbook available in America, and the most popular at that time, was Hannah Glasse's *The Art of Cookery Made Plain and Easy*. Originally published in England in 1747, one copy published in Alexandria, Virginia, came out in 1805, with a reprint in 1812, still very British in concept but billed as a new edition with modern improvements. Glasse includes a bill of fare similar to Carter's, with three courses instead of two and "several new receipts adapted to the American mode of cooking," many of which are the same as the ones that appeared in Carter's 1803 appendix.

Glasse included recipes not just for cooking but also ones such as "the famous Thieves Vinegar, which can be used to rinse the mouth, wash under the arm pits, neck and shoulder…and feet." This was a successful cookbook with helpful information, assuming the cook knew a lot of basic cooking techniques. Many recipes were short and to the point, and following a recipe did not necessarily produce the same results every time a dish was made. To re-create a recipe of our earliest pioneers, one would have to take into consideration differences in the foods then and now. Today, fruits, vegetables and farm animals are bigger and bred for better taste or made more durable for easier shipping without as much spoilage. Leavening agents such as eggs were smaller, while yeast and pearl ash were used because baking soda and baking powder were not yet available. Sea salt had a saltier flavor than the table salt so often used today. Dairy products were raw, and the homemade butter was usually heavily salted.

In 1796, Amelia Simmons published a cookbook, *American Cookery*, in part by substituting American ingredients for British ones. The second edition, written by "an American orphan," as Amelia Simmons referred to herself, was printed the same year as the first in order to correct the mistakes—what she considered "adulterations"—made by the publisher. Reprinted over a dozen times, it was a widely accepted book and, as stated on the cover of the book, "adapted to this country, and all grades of life."

By the time Florida became a territory in 1821, colonial cookbooks were more available to the settlers moving into the area, despite being somewhat isolated from the rest of the country. With an expanded use of garden greens and herbs, along with butter, cream, beef, chicken and honey, new recipes were being forged. Considered too costly or unavailable for most in the backwoods, cookbooks, pottery and china dishes were becoming more common in towns. Tallahassee, Jacksonville, Key West, Saint Joseph, Tampa, Apalachicola and many other towns along waterways were developing throughout the state. Many boundaries we know today were established in the early nineteenth century.

Science and technology were on the rise, and this helped to change the way people cooked. Kitchens were improving, with better quality and more variety of pots, pans, dishes, cutlery, tablecloths and napkins. General stores provided commercially prepared canned food and out-of-town newspapers, and farmers could trade their vegetables, eggs and butter for sacks or barrels of sugar, flour, molasses and vinegar. Items were taken home in cone-shaped paper, baskets, sacks, bags, clay pots and jars. Spices, coffee beans and sugar were in large bins, and crackers were shipped and displayed in barrels. Imported tea and chocolate were available for some, but the majority of people moving into the Sunshine State were too poor or too far from a general store to acquire the newest foods or cooking supplies. Additional produce such as lettuce, tomatoes, parsley, radishes, cucumbers, celery and cabbage was provided by the kitchen garden, if one was lucky enough to have one.

Some of the basics supplies of the poor included an axe, shovel, tongs, frying pans, kettles, pots, bowls, plates and tableware, while those somewhat

This photograph of the interior of a general store and post office in Hialeah was taken in 1921.

better off added milk pails, sieves, jugs, churns, spinning wheels, bake pans, wooden bowls and coffee mills, with the even more prosperous adding butchering knives, a sausage gun, funnels, a vinegar press, earthenware, brass and copperware along with pewter, silver, porcelain, china and glass ware. Kitchenware items featured at the Constitutional Convention State Museum in Port Saint Joe include a mortar and pestle, a butter churn, an ornate stove with spindle legs, cast-iron spiders and Dutch ovens.

The early colonists were just as dependent on corn as a vital staple as the early settlers of Florida were. They, too, imitated the Native Indians in scraping kernels from their cobs with seashells or bones. When times were hard, it was not uncommon to eat some form of corn three times a day in a variety of ways: fresh, dried or (commonly) ground into cornmeal. *America's First Cuisines*, by Sophie Coe, sums it up by saying corn "could be eaten at many stages of its development...very young maize ears chewed up husk, silk, cob and all...is tender, succulent and sweet...a few weeks (later)...green maize, either roasted in the husk or boiled" is a delicacy. To make grinding easier, the dried kernels of corn were soaked with wood ashes to remove the transparent skin before cooking. Dating as far back as 1500 BC, this method also improves the nutritional value of the corn. Lacking most fruits and vegetables during the winter months, resourceful women brought variety to meals by using cornmeal to make a wide selection of breads, puddings, pancakes and pies. Leftover cornmeal porridge was sliced and fried for breakfast. A popular old Indian method was to create a pudding featuring molasses, butter and spices. This historic colonial dish is still served today at Durgin Park, in Boston, and it tastes as good as it sounds.

Cookbooks began to feature more detailed recipes and step-by-step instructions, along with standards of measurement. The new cast-iron plow of 1819 gave way to the steel plow of 1837, and Cyrus McCormick, the "Father of Modern Agriculture," gave us the McCormick reaper, which made planting and harvesting a little easier. Major changes were underway that would improve the eating habits of Floridians. Changes in procurement and preparation of food resulted in greater variety and better-tasting foods. Many of the same foods we eat today were being served, but the preparation techniques differed and were based on tools available at the time. Improved farming from crop rotation—something the Indians had been doing for years—along with the building of fences and controlled breeding led to more higher-quality foods. Timesaving gristmills were introduced to the rural areas of Florida to grind the wheat into flour and corn into meal. Breakfast and dinner were the main meals of the day, usually followed by a light supper before retiring for the evening. Preservation of foods without refrigeration meant more salting and drying of foods, home canning and pickling. In the early 1800s, pork was preserved by smoking because salt was expensive.

Land grants brought more people, and cowmen brought large herds to start a new life under primitive conditions. Most of the Florida settlers discovered life in the wild scrub of Florida's backwoods to be difficult and harsh. Steamboats eventually cruised the rivers of Florida, serving as floating general stores, bringing food and supplies. As the Industrial Revolution in the 1830s brought less expensive culinary equipment, more affordable items were being sold to the new settlers, but not on a large scale. Some were pioneers of Florida and others outlaws, both living off the land. Railroads were beginning to operate, with plans to extend to the remote regions of the state.

Cooking in the fireplace, with the help of a reflecting oven, or cooking meat on a hand-turned spit were replaced with wood-burning stoves or brick ovens. No more roasting by the fire, meats were then "oven-roasted" or baked. However, these ovens were not used on a widespread basis due to cost and

Gristmills like this one, located in Calhoun County in the early 1900s, helped to lessen the work load for those fortunate enough to have access to them.

availability. With no temperature controls, using ovens may have been more convenient but yielded uneven results, so cooks had to make educated guesses based on prior experience. Cookbooks at the time did not give temperatures. As kitchens and equipment became more sophisticated, roasting and better temperature control resulted in better flavors. Reading and writing were an important part of passing on recipes from one generation to another, but oral traditions continued to be common practice for most Floridians at that time.

Mary Randolph wrote one of the most influential American cookbooks at the time, *The Virginia Housewife or, Methodical Cook*, in 1824. Reprinted numerous times over the next forty years, her title page includes the simple statement, "Method is the soul of management." Influenced by Glasse, with an attention to detail, Randolph was also known for her excellent cooking. Her recipes reflected regional produce and cooking practices, with an English influence, creating a whole new style of cooking: southern. Known for her hospitality in the area, in the kitchen, her multicultural recipes reflected ethnic dishes.

For the novice cook, her suggestions could make the difference between a delicious meal and a disaster. To cure bacon, she states, "Hogs are in the highest perfection, from two and half, to four years old, and make the best bacon." She offers more information on weight, feed and market distance, before describing the technique. As Glasse and Simmons did, Randolph, too, included directions for dressing a turtle and mock turtle soup, noting the time of day to kill the turtle and start the soup. Her American southern recipes were also influenced by American Indian and African slave dishes with catfish, tomatoes, squash, sweet potatoes, eggplant and field peas, which would help to make these dishes more acceptable to Florida cooks at that time. Corn, sweet potatoes, squash, beans, fruits and nuts of the Indian culture, along with contributions from the plantation slaves such as field peas, eggplant, yams and tomatoes, often were combined with other ingredients to create new dishes.

The American Frugal Housewife, by Mrs. Lydia Marie Child, with over two dozen reprints from 1829 to 1850, morphed from Carter's book and was at first titled *The Frugal Housewife*. However, this was the same as the title of a similar English work, so she changed the title to *The American Frugal Housewife* to avoid conflict with the English book. Child gave homemaking and health advice and went one step further, saying her book was "dedicated to those who are not ashamed of Economy." She states, "I have attempted to teach how money can be saved, not how it can be enjoyed." But she still helped lay the foundation for southern cooking with her fried chicken, gravy and catsup along with instructions on how to salt and pack pork. Yet her advice, "Economical people will seldom use preserves, except for sickness," would disappoint many a southern diner at the dinner table. Child provided tips on making coffee using substitutes such as dry brown bread, rye grain or roasted peas but goes on to say they do not make a good substitute and that you are better off going without. She gives details on roasting, almost burning and grinding French coffee, which she considers extravagant unless you have boarders. Her refinements for coffee included adding fish skin, salt pork, butter, egg shells and egg whites for various reasons, but she notes they are not necessary if you are prudent. Boiled milk she used as a substitute for cream, which would give results similar to the steamed milk so often used today.

Tomes of household management and cookery books were being published. These domestic manuals were written with a scientific approach to home economics, today known as "Family and Consumer Science." Ruth Schwartz Cowan's research for her book *More Work for Mother* indicates the "housewife is expected to perform work that ranges from the most menial physical labor to the most abstract of mental manipulations and to do it all without any specialized training." *A Treatise on Domestic Economy*, by Catharine Esther Beecher, published around the time Florida attained statehood, reflects some of the difficulties of household management, mainly serving meals. Beecher stated that the book was "dedicated to American Mothers whose intelligence and virtues have inspired admiration and respect whose experience has furnished many valuable suggestions," later noting that "young girls, especially in the more wealthy classes, are not trained for their profession." (Catharine Beecher was the sister-in-law of Harriett Beecher Stowe, who owned an orange grove in central Florida in 1846.)

Mrs. Beeton's Book of Cookery and Household Management, written in England while the Civil War was beginning in the United States, is still in print today, with American notes and practical advice for homemakers. She wanted to pass on the knowledge of previous generations in one volume but also to simplify the recipes by using a list of ingredients followed by the mode of preparation, number of servings and seasonality of the dish. Later, *The Fannie Farmer Cookbook* and *The Joy of Cooking* would set a standard for American cooking.

By the turn of the twentieth century, regional cookbooks were becoming available, such as the *Florida Tropical Cook Book* published in 1912 and edited by the Aid Society of the First Presbyterian Church of Miami, Florida. It sold for $1.50, and the advertisements, used to offset the cost of publication, tell a story all their own. One ad promoted the Florida Everglades as the only "truly tropical section of the United States" with property for sale. Another bank "welcomes women's accounts of which it has a goodly number." The one for Florida arrowroot from the Little River factory explains it's "The world's best culinary starch. No chemicals used in manufacturing." Books such as this one were helpful in introducing new residents to information on some of the ingredients they had never seen or used before. "In offering this book to the public, we feel that we are giving 'in a nut shell' results of successful years of experience with local fruits, fish and vegetables, and trust that it will contribute to the welfare and comfort of every home it enters." The recipes were originals, standards and old family favorites, and pioneer women of Florida tested all the recipes.

A classic Florida cookbook still in print today was written by Marjorie Kinnan Rawlings, author of *Cross Creek* and *Cross Creek Cookery*, first published in 1942. It reads like one of her stories, with recipes throughout the book. Describing what it was like living on her orange grove at Cross Creek with her cow Dora and her cook Idella, the book is funny and fun to read. Some of the recipes are original, and others are borrowed, such as the first one in the book for "Mrs. Chancey's Spanish Bean Soup" from the Tampa mayor's wife. With menus for breakfast, lunch and dinner, a great many of the recipes

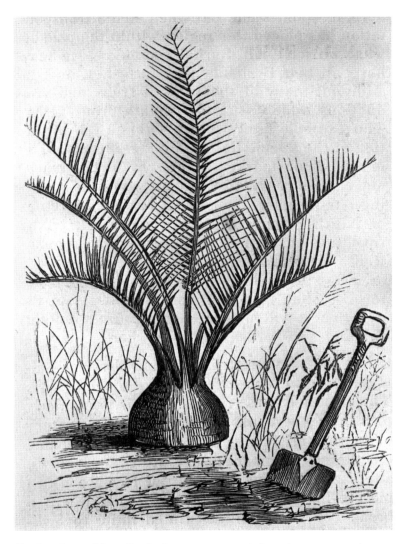

Crackers learned from Seminoles to extract starch from the arrowroot plant by first beating it to a pulp and then soaking, straining and allowing it to settle before draining, washing again and drying in the sun.

are based on Florida ingredients, as it showcases the true essence of regional cooking. She offered three versions for the preparation of swamp cabbage: using the thinly sliced white cylinder with a French dressing; boiled with bacon, salt and pepper, similar to the dish served at the Swamp Cabbage Festival in LaBelle; or boiled with butter, cream and salt.

The dining room at the Marjorie Kinnan Rawlings Historic State Park can be seen during ranger-led tours on a seasonal basis. The house and farmyard are designated as a National Historic Landmark, now a part of the Florida State Park system.

A 1950s community cookbook, published in Tallahassee by the local garden club, *Camellia Cookery*, showcases not only foods from the area but also multicultural dishes from around the state. A Spanish bean soup recipe is featured, very different from the *Cross Creek* version, using Minorcan Datil peppers. Greek classics such as moussaka and pastitso are featured along with grits, grits and more grits. More than one recipe for hush puppies and spoon bread are included, as is a recipe for using venison. The picciadia recipe, now called picadillo, comes with an explanation: "I must give all credit to my husband's mother, Mrs. E.E. Crusoe Jr. of Bartow, Florida, for teaching me to prepare the above recipe. It is of Cuban origin and she, and her mother before her, used it in Key West." Some of the recipes are handwritten and signed by the creator and others typed out. On the humorous side, "How to Preserve a Husband" and "a recipe for pleasant listening" are included in an ad for the local radio station.

7

Seminole, Southern, Soul and Cracker Cooking

The mixing of Seminole, southern, soul and Cracker cooking was the end of colonial cooking and the beginning of a new Florida cuisine. The Civil War and three Seminole Wars changed the face and food supply of Florida. While the Seminoles found their way to the Florida Everglades, plantation owners and pioneers settled the rest of the state. In his book *Hogmeat and Hoecake*, Sam B. Hilliard, describes the food supply of the South, from 1840 to 1860, as a region feeding itself. Self-sufficient settlers killed game, caught fish, slaughtered livestock, sowed corn and grew vegetables, in addition to the daily chores of feeding chickens and tending to the cattle or hogs they owned. Plantations, utilizing slave labor for their cooks and kitchen help, were established across the state until the end of the Civil War.

There were more Cracker farmers than plantation owners in antebellum Florida, but they had little influence or power, so they worked their fields in hopes of making a better life for themselves. Since Cracker and soul cooking were born out of necessity, Crackers used what they could eke out of the backwoods wilderness of Florida, many times with the help of Seminoles. After lavish meals were prepared for plantation dinner tables, slaves depended on what they could rustle up to serve in their slave quarters. Just as the combination of Seminole and Cracker cooking is reflected in some classic old Florida recipes, the British influence on plantation cooking, and the skills of the slaves working in the kitchens, produced some of the greatest recipes in America during this tumultuous period. As difficult as that time was, "to throw out the superlative dishes of the colonial and antebellum periods because of their association with slavery would be to ignore the creative genius of generations of black cooks, and thus to discredit one of the truly outstanding achievements in American social history," wrote John Egerton in *Southern Food*. The unique cooking styles that emerged are still practiced today.

Written in 1881 by former slave Abby Fisher, *What Mrs. Fisher Knows about Old Southern Cooking, Soups, Pickles, Preserves, Etc.* has the distinction of being the first cookbook written by an African American. Her recipes are in sharp contrast to the typical diet of a slave, but they reflect her African heritage and plantation-style cooking brought together in a delicious combination. Based on experience from over thirty-five years of cooking in the South, many of her recipes are considered classic southern dishes today. Recipes include roast venison, roast pig, a variety of croquettes, fried chicken, watermelon rind pickles, gumbos, pies and cakes.

Distinct cooking styles were developing in the newly christened state of Florida, and new gadgets and cooking styles eventually seeped into the homes and hearths of Florida kitchens. Seminoles had a separate chickee for cooking, but for others, the outdoor brick ovens and fireplaces, fitted with an iron rod across the top for suspending kettles and pots, were replaced by a wood-burning cast-iron stove. By the turn of the century, iceboxes and electricity emerged and an array of modern cooking appliances was introduced. The first U.S. patent for mechanical refrigeration was granted in 1851, to physician John Gorrie, of Apalachicola. One hundred years later, air conditioning had a profound impact on the future of Floridians. By the 1860s, cookbooks addressed the issues of both open-hearth and iron-stove cooking. The skill of combining new flavors and creating new dishes was left to the cook or homemaker, but the kitchen was full of the proper resources to accomplish the job.

Today, some of the former plantation sites are parts of state and national parks, such as the Kingsley Plantation on Fort George Island, in Jacksonville. Established in the early 1800s and run by former slave, Anna Madgigine Jai Kingsley, after her marriage to a white man, Zephaniah Kingsley, the self-sustaining sugarcane plantation produced enough food for those living there, as did many plantations at the time. The largest meal of the day was the midday meal, called dinner; the smaller evening meal was called supper. It was not uncommon for a plantation dinner to include four or five kinds of meat and a large variety of vegetables and desserts. There were also breads and rolls served with butter, preserves and jelly.

In the mid-1800s, Major Robert Gamble established a 3,500-acre sugarcane plantation, now Gamble Plantation Historic State Park, near

Plantation cooking was often done at the fireplace, like the one shown here in the kitchen of the Kinglsey Plantation, today a part of the National Park Service on Fort George Island.

Ellenton. By 1845, many sugar plantations in the area were distilling sugar and molasses from the cane plant for shipment to the New Orleans market. Gamble noted in an agriculture circular of 1851, "The fruit culture of my immediate district is confined to the production of oranges, lemons, limes, guavas, bananas, pineapples, cocoanuts, etc." These foods are still associated with Florida today.

A thriving sugar plantation and the limestone-hewn Yulee Sugar Mill owned by David Levy Yulee was located near the Homosassa River. Sugar cane could not be economically shipped to a mill, so each plantation had its own equipment for removing juice and cooking the cane into sugar. A grapefruit plantation in the 1880s, named Saint Helena, in Pinellas County, established by the French Count Odet Philippe, led to the spread of citrus into Hillsborough County. Philippe is considered the first European settler in Pinellas County and was also the first to cultivate grapefruit in Florida. Philippe was later inducted into the Florida Citrus Hall of Fame for his contributions to the citrus industry. In addition to grapefruit, he planted a variety of citrus and other fruits such as oranges, limes, avocados, pears and bananas, which he had acquired in the Caribbean. His was the first post-

Plantation owners often hosted Fourth of July barbecues for slaves, roasting whole hogs, similar to this 1886 one at a Masonic picnic in Kissimmee.

colonial commercial grove, and the area is now a part of Philippe Park near Safety Harbor, also known for its historic Indian mounds.

Through Some Eventful Years, written by Susan Bradford Eppes and published in 1926, recalls her childhood days on the Tallahassee Pine Hill Plantation, before and during the Civil War. The 1850s annual barbecue at the plantation, on the Fourth of July, for "black folks, several hundred, no white folks allowed" was one event described by Eppes. "Ever so many deep pits had been dug and all night fires had been burning in these pits, fires made of oak-wood (for pine would spoil the taste). Over these pits of glowing coals green hickory saplings had been placed and the cooks for the day were busily engaged in putting into the pits whole beeves (beef), many of them; whole hogs, I dare not say how many…Later in the day bread would be baked, potatoes roasted, coffee made; already jugs of milk and watermelons without number had been sunk in the cool depths of a nearby stream."

As a part of the Federal Writers' Project in the 1930s, former slaves were interviewed about their lives on the plantations in antebellum times. Many from the state of Florida contributed to this body of work, providing details of everyday meals and special-occasion splurges. Christine Mitchell tells how biscuits replaced cornbread on Sunday mornings. For the most part, slaves raised their own food in vegetable gardens and home-cured meats in the smokehouse. Some ate what the plantation owner and his family had, while others lived on a diet of mostly cornbread, bacon, beans, peas, rice, sweet potatoes and greens. Coffee was sometimes imitation and made of parched corn. Drinking water was drawn from an open well, using a gourd or tin cup for dipping. When allowed, fishing became a favorite vocation, and some slaves established themselves as small merchants of seafood. Others tended to small provisional gardens to supplement their daily fare, and a few became highly successful farmers.

Acie Thomas describes how slave children waded in the streams, fished, chased rabbits and always knew where the choicest wild berries and nuts grew. Eggs found from stray hens, turkeys, guineas and geese were wrapped in wet rags, covered with ashes and roasted in remote corners of the plantation. "When they were done, a loud pop announced the fact to the roaster." For dinner, potatoes and sweet potatoes were cooked in the same manner, often without the rags, and cornbread was mixed, wrapped in large leaves and then placed in the hot coals till parched.

Salt was obtained by evaporating seawater or procured, by the barrel, from the closest saltworks . The preservation qualities of salt made it essential for survival since refrigeration was still years away. Salt absorbs moisture that can grow bacteria and also changes the chemical composition of meat in much the same way cooking does. The saltworks in Florida were created just in time for use in the Civil War, with the largest operations in northwest Florida. Collecting seawater in large iron pots and boiling it until the water evaporated leaves behind white crystals of salt. The saltworks at Saint Andrews Bay, Apalachicola, south to Cedar Key and Tampa Bay, provided seasonal salt for preserving meat. The Saint Andrews Bay Saltworks was one of the largest producers of salt in the South. Salt was an important war commodity, and many men were exempted from combat in order to maintain the saltworks.

Dining habits across the state changed due to lack of provisions during the war and the need to send as much food as possible to the men and boys in battle. Those at home ate what was left. Although it was repetitious at times, fresh fruits and vegetables, which would spoil by the time they reached the army, were usually eaten by those at home. Eppes sums it up: "Dishes of broiled or baked chickens or roast of mutton, for that was a meat which we could not send, except to nearby camps; delicious batter bread, hot, with fresh butter; vegetables, daintily prepared, maybe with sweet potato pone…On rare occasion a cake made of brown sugar, or syrup…and cut glass bowls filled with custard, also made with brown sugar and flavored, usually, with leaves

Hundreds of saltworks, such as this one on Saint Andrews Bay, were located along the Gulf Coast before being destroyed during the Civil War. *Photographed by Joy Sheffield Harris.*

from the nearest peach-tree…(when cake was lacking) pans of syrup bread took its place. Baked eggs were always liked and salad could easily be had, for we made our own vinegar in great abundance from fruit juices."

The smokehouse was full of hams, sausage, pickled pigs feet and corned beef, to be prepared as needed. But flour was difficult to come by, so "egg bread" made a good substitute for those times when troops stopped by. "Such piling dishes and plates of fried sweet potatoes, eggs ad libitum, fried with ham, scrambled with butter, boiled hard and served with crisp lettuce, green and fresh; milk in abundance, even for that crowd and the dinner ended with fritters and pancakes, with plenty of delicious Florida Syrup," Eppes recounts.

After the war, boiled eggs and batter bread were common on the Eppes's Pine Hill Plantation and often the only foods available. Later, Eppes mentions "salt rising" bread and food sent over by others. "They must have 'Heard her cry in the land of pie' for cousin Peggy sent a beautiful sponge cake this afternoon, and Hattie sent a leg of mutton beautifully browned all ready to be eaten." But broiled chicken, fragrant coffee, hot biscuits and fresh butter were much more common.

Many of the recipes mentioned by Eppes are classic antebellum dishes, and several are described in the cookbook *Dishes and Beverage of the Old South*, by Martha McCulloch-Williams. This book was written after the Civil War but based on her childhood memories of plantation cooking from her seat on the "biscuit block" in the detached kitchen, thirty yards from the house. McCulloch-Williams writes that there is no magic to good cooking, but "bad cooking can ruin the very best of raw food stuffs, all the art of all the cooks in the world can do no more than palliate things stale, flat and unprofitable. Food must satisfy the palate else it will never truly satisfy the stomach." She had high standards for cooks, referring to cooking sherry as an abomination and declaring, "You will never get out of pot or pan anything fundamentally better than what went into it." She speculates, "I wonder, now and then, if the prevalence of divorce has any connection with the decline of home cooking?" In her opinion, "The one-piece dinner is as convenient and comfortable as the one-piece frock…the piece de resistance."

True to southern tastes, the cooking style, she recalled, had "a free hand at the fat, the sweet, strong waters and high flavors." Her description of the kitchen recalls knives stuck in cracks; hand-wrought forks; spoons; ladles and skimmers hung on nails; two- to ten-gallon cast-iron pots, with close-fitting tops; ovens deep and shallow; spiders; skillets; tea kettles; stew kettles; a broiler, with a long spider-legged trivet; a hoe-baker; a biscuit baker; waffle irons, with legs like tongs; and hollow-ware with lids. "Periodically every piece was burned out, turned upside down over a roaring fire and left there until red hot, then slowly cooled. This burning out left a fine smooth surface after scouring. Cast iron, being in a degree porous, necessarily took up traces of food when it had been used for cooking a month or so." Using a shovel, live coals were spread upon the hearth and then iron vessels were set above the smoothly spread-out coals. Other pots were swung over the fire and heated before being set in place and covered with a blanket of coals and embers. She recounts brown-bag cooking and the way the sealed and loaded bag must be laid on a grate-shelf in a hot oven, being careful not to touch the hot iron, as this could be fatal to the dish. She felt it was easier to prepare vegetables this way, rather than on top of the stove.

The Reconstruction Era, following the Civil War, brought many changes to the lifestyle of Floridians. Southern food production for domestic consumption was insufficient, and getting food was difficult. Without the help of slave labor, the plantations could not function, and many small farmers came home to ruined farms. The Homestead Act of 1862, along with the creation of the Department of Agriculture, encouraged more pioneers to set up homesteads. Staking a 160-acre claim required living on the land for five years while improving it. At the same time, livestock roamed the woods and the cow hunters (called cowmen or cattlemen, but not cowboys) branded and claimed what roamed free. Pioneer farming in rural Florida was an attractive proposition, with free fertile land, wild game to hunt and abundant fishing. The homesteaders came in covered wagons, on horseback or on mules or ox-carts; sometimes they even came in sailboats or by foot, all to settle in the Sunshine State. These settlers became known as Crackers, and in order to survive, they worked hard. Rustling cattle seemed to be a lifestyle many enjoyed.

The Cracker culture has roots in the Celtic way of life. Migrating to the area from New England, these Scots-Irish found they had more in common with the southern way of life than that of New England. According to Grady McWhiney, author of *Cracker Culture: Celtic Ways in the Old South*, "Traditionally, neither Celts nor Southerners like sheep," and open-range herding was another practice they both used. New England was like a home away from home for the English, while the South was a second home for the Scots-Irish. Today, a Florida Cracker is best known as someone born and raised in the Sunshine State. According to some, the name has it origins in the cracking of the cowhunter's whip, but the term was used as early as the 1790s by Spanish officials.

Many new settlers lived in thatch huts, similar to the Native American chickees, while some built modest log cabins with uncovered openings in the place of doors and windows. A sweet potato patch often served as the garden. Fishing and hunting brought in more food, and corn would eventually become the staple of the Cracker diet, but many times sweet potatoes were the only item on the dinner table. From Native Americans, Crackers learned seasonality and edibility of plants and how to live off the land by utilizing coontie, prickly pear, cabbage palm, poke salad, palm berries, hickory nuts, acorns and wild berries. South Florida was sparsely settled, but cattle ranching was expanding throughout the rest of the state. Tampa became the shipping point for one thousand head of cattle per month. North Florida homesteads might have grape arbors, citrus, peaches, pears and figs. Subsistence farming became more common, with farmers growing corn, potatoes, tomatoes and lettuce and tending to a few cattle, chickens and hogs.

George M. Barbour wrote *Florida for Tourists, Invalids, and Settlers* and told of the poor "crackers" he encountered while touring the newly settled regions of the state. He did not think very highly of the "grub boxes" they set up for cooking fish or tortoise along with "a chunk of fat side-pork; this, and a cupful of boiled 'grits' or hominy, with molasses for sauce and a cup of coffee." Fried salt pork was a staple for many and at times referred to as "Poor Man's Chicken" when boiled, drained and dredged in cornmeal before frying. The barnyard chicken was a luxury until food became industrialized and brought the price of chicken down. Reserved for special occasions, the chicken was caught, cleaned and fried immediately or boiled in a perloo. Occasionally, neighbors would get together for a celebration that might include dancing, singing, games and contests. These special gatherings required special meals, and the Cracker-style perloo (also know as pilau, with a variety of other spellings) would be created in large pots over open fires in which chicken was boiled with rice and other ingredients to feed the crowd of hungry neighbors.

Barbour was not a fan of Cracker cooking and described the harsh lifestyle, explaining how game was shot and traded for flour, sugar and grits. When food was more plentiful, "women did the baking and invited all the crackers for miles around…guava jelly…heaped on table…sweet potatoes (undercooked), baked or fried…bread (just hot steamy dough in a burned crust)…fat pork…muddy coffee (plenty of grounds for being muddy, if the reader will excuse my pun…)."

The cast-iron skillet was one essential for Cracker cooking. After years of use, it develops a smooth black surface, used for cooking a large variety of foods. Wooden bowls for biscuit making were common, but a meat grinder for making sausage was considered a luxury. In order to have year-round fruits and vegetables, home canning became a way of life, and that trend continued for decades after the Civil War. Smokehouses for meats were used to store these foods for long periods of time. The kitchen was often yards from the house, but new equipment changed to meet the needs of new kitchens and cooking methods.

Cookbooks included more than recipes. They provided household hints and economic strategies for living on less, especially helpful in the South after the Civil War. Commercially canned foods were becoming more common, and thanks to John L. Mason, canning with self-sealing lids on reusable glass jars made pickling and preserving a little easier and safer for the home cook. In sharp contrast to the earlier *Virginia Housewife*, written at a time of plenty on the southern plantation, the *Confederate Receipt Book* was published to help out with the shortages that resulted from the war. It gave cooks ideas on how to make do with what they could get, since what they were accustomed to was no longer available. Fewer than thirty pages, it includes tips, remedies

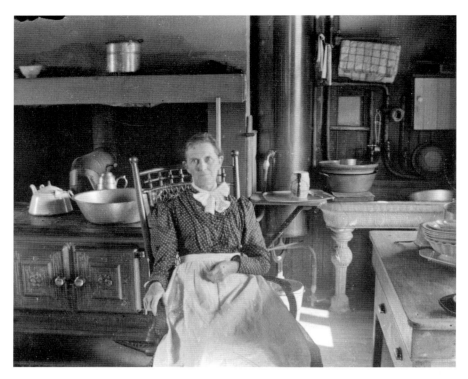

This Cracker kitchen in Melrose was functional and practical.

and suggestions in cookery and housewifery, with basic recipes for biscuits, breads and puddings. Some not-so-basic recipes are included as well, such as one for artificial oysters made from green corn, eggs, flour, butter, salt and pepper, or apple pie without apples, using sweetened crackers, with butter and nutmeg for flavoring. Molasses was used as a substitute for rationed sugar; as a byproduct of sugar processing, it was easier to acquire. A simple recipe for "Indian Bread" is included using buttermilk, cornmeal and molasses, three basic but important food sources of the South at that time. Other tips included using roasted acorns steeped in boiling water as a substitute for coffee and egg whites as a substitute for cream.

After the devastation of the war, many women turned to writing, both cookbooks and literature. Arabella P. Hill wrote *Mrs. Hill's New Cook Book*, which included household hints and medicinal tips, reflecting a change in the style of living for those accustomed to having slaves or servants. Also included were recipes for ground pea candy, fig preserves, arrowroot sauce and muscadines. The thick-skinned, bronze-colored scuppernong, a type of muscadine grape, grows wild in many parts of Florida. As a summer-to-early-fall snack, they could be plucked from the climbing vine and eaten on the spot. Just chew while separating the seeds and skin from the pulp, and spit the seeds and skin out. They were a precious treat for a child playing outside to come upon and, as Harper Lee wrote in *To Kill A Mockingbird*, "helping ourselves to someone's scuppernongs was part of our ethical culture, but money was different." Scuppernongs are the larger green variety of the muscadine. The South's muscadine grape ripens as individual grapes on the cluster, like the sea grape.

Other parts of the country were discovering rural Florida through the writings of Harriet Beecher Stowe and her book *Palmetto Leaves*, with stories centered on her orange grove and winter home on a bluff overlooking the Saint Johns River, in Mandarin. Stowe and her family spent their winters in Florida starting in 1872. She described the scent of orange blossoms as having "a stimulating effect on our nerves—a sort of dreamy intoxication," describing the beautiful orange groves with their "stately orange tree, thirty feet high with spreading, graceful top and varnished green leaves, full of golden fruit." She told of Indian raids and shooting gators, but she also introduced the charming state to a whole new group of wealthy people who came to visit and chose to stay and make a home in the sparsely populated Sunshine State. Finding a cook proved to be a challenge, as she declares the extent and knowledge of their cooking was to mix meal with water and salt for hoecakes and to fry salt pork or ham or chicken. She describes catching fish for dinner: A hole is "dug in the smooth white sand; and a fire of dry light wood is merrily crackling therein…the fire has burned low, and the sand-hole is thoroughly heated…great broad bonnet-leaves" are used to double-line the hole, and the fish are baked clambake style. When removed, "the whole external part of the fish—scales, skin, and fins—comes off, leaving the meat white and pure, and deliciously juicy."

Settlers moved farther south with small herds of family cows while others were setting up homesteads with the promise of branding and claiming the cattle that roamed free at the time. By the late 1880s, these Cracker homesteads were beginning to show some progress and hope for a better tomorrow. Barbed-wire fence led to better control of cattle, and large-scale commercial agriculture introduced new crops to the state. They planted, harvested, cooked, baked, canned and preserved.

With the commercial development of baking powder and baking soda in the 1880s, biscuits took their place beside cornbread at the table. For decades after the Civil War, Floridians still dried, salted, pickled, potted, canned,

Harriett Beecher Stowe is seated with family in front of their home at Mandarin during the late 1800s.

jelled and jammed foods as a practical, economical and delicious way to enjoy the bounty of their harvest—although time consuming, they had more time than money. Year in and year out, they made their own bread, churned butter, milked cows, ground sausage and gathered eggs from the chicken coop. Seasonal changes brought variety to the table as they collected nuts and berries and supplemented their dining options by hunting and fishing.

The telephone, phonograph and the light bulb, as well as the growth of the meatpacking industry, was aided by new means of transportation and refrigerated rail cars for perishables. Changes included a shift from living off the land to dependence on the community and others for products such as white flour, canned milk, fruits, vegetables and cured meat. By the turn of the twentieth century, canned goods were standard, and recipes called for them. Bakeries and grocery stores would soon appear in every city neighborhood, and mail-order catalogues were on their way to rural areas.

In the 1880s, the new term "week-end" was coined, and germs were discovered. *Common Sense in the Household: A Manual of Practical Housewifery* by Marion Harland was published, dedicated to "fellow-housekeepers, North, East, South and West" who do their own work. She strove to make "the collection of family receipts more intelligible and available," noting that failure is the stepping-stone to success and that "method, skill, economy in the kitchen, depends so much of the well-being of the rest of the household...(and is the) foundation of housewifery."

The Dixie Cook-Book, by Estelle Woods Wilcox, is another tome of recipes and household tips written in 1883. It is dedicated to the mothers, wives and daughters of the "sunny south." From bread-making to dress-making, it's more than a cookbook. With a chemistry section included, it's also a bible for southern homemaking. Promoting her book with the statement, "Blunders in cookery cost money, and it is a self-evident fact that a few spoiled dishes represent the price of a good cookbook," she goes on to say some of the cookbooks of the past featured authors who were good book-makers but poor bread-makers.

By the 1890s, settlers living in cabins with detached kitchens might also have a barn, a smokehouse for curing meats, livestock pens, kitchen gardens, cane syrup grinders and a well and pump, if they were not located near a spring. The barn or lean-to shed stored the grain, canned goods, root vegetables, cured meats and homemade wine. The kitchen garden provided tomatoes, greens, cabbage and both white and sweet potatoes. When children went to school, lunch was carried in a bucket or tied up in a cloth; some common items carried to school were sweet potatoes, rice, meat, grits, hard-boiled eggs and biscuits or cornbread with syrup.

In the spring, the corn, cane and vegetables were planted, and the women were still the ones to cook, bake, can, churn butter, slop hogs, shell peas, shuck corn and milk cows. A hand pump in the kitchen, using shared gourds or metal dippers for drinking, was a convenience not everyone shared. Fresh milk was strained through a sieve and set in a screened cabinet to cool and allow the cream rise to the top. Before refrigeration, the milk might have been kept in a cool well or placed in a screened cage and hung from the branch of a shade tree. To keep brush fires at bay, the yard was swept clean outside of the house.

The fall tradition of harvesting and grinding sugarcane took on a festive atmosphere, ending with the much-anticipated cane boil for syrup on

In the late 1800s, sugar cane grinding was hard work and usually a community affair. Some worked the fields cutting the cane and loaded it on the cart to be carried to others at the grinding machine.

both the plantation and in the Cracker community. Cane grinding on the plantation provided enough syrup and cane juice "for everyone to enjoy." The mule- or ox-drawn cane press slowly turned to extract the juice as the animal hitched to a pole walked in a circle. The juice was boiled in a kettle to just the right consistency for cane syrup. When the color changed from amber to dark brown, the sweet syrup was nearly finished. It takes about one hundred gallons of juice to produce one gallon of syrup. Cane syrup was stored in mason jars or cans and provided a substitute for sugar. The animal-drawn cane press was replaced with the gasoline engine by 1910, with rollers to press and squeeze juice from the cane stalks.

The cool fall weather was a perfect time for social gatherings and a good old-fashioned hog killing. The meat was shared, due to lack of refrigeration, and the process took a few strong men. After the hog was shot, it was put into a huge vat of scalding hot water to loosen and help remove the bristles on its skin. The skin was saved for cracklings and pork rinds. The meat was then cut into sections, salted and hung to dry in the chimney or smokehouse. Nothing went to waste—the fat was used to flavor vegetables when cooking, the tail was skinned and chopped for stew, the bones for soups, the brains were fried, the hooves were boiled for jelly and the feet were pickled. The heart and liver were also eaten. "From snout to tail, the pig was a walking meat market," writes Egerton. And as they say in the South, "the only thing left was the squeal." Harland provides her impression of pork in the South: "Where, in spite of the warm climate, the consumption of pork is double that of the North, the full-grown hog is seldom represented by any of his parts at the table, fresh or pickled, unless it be during killing-time, when fresh spare-ribs, chine and steak, with other succulent bits, are welcome upon the choicest bills of fare."

Old-fashioned bacon and ham were made by packing in salt or soaking in a strong salt brine, turning, re-salting and draining frequently, for several weeks to a month, until the salt is soaked through and the meat cured. Then, it is slowly smoked, until darker in color, with the taste of smoke throughout the meat. Salt is a preservative that stops the growth of molds and bacteria, and smoke, also a preservative, was necessary without refrigeration.

Corn continued to be the staff of life, used as feed for livestock as well as for human consumption. It was husked, shelled and eaten at the time of harvest or cooked in soups and stews, made into creamed corn or served as corn on the cob. Dried corn was pounded into grits or cornmeal to make pone, hoecakes or cornbread, with the leftover grain used as chicken feed. Later, with a gristmill, the process was much easier as a large waterwheel turned huge granite stones that ground the corn into meal or grits. Often used as breading on other foods, cornmeal became a staple of Cracker cooking.

8
Rivers, Rails, Resorts, Restaurants and Regions

Juxtaposed against the struggle and hardship of rural Florida after the Civil War, the Gilded Age brought glamorous winter resorts and lavish mansions to the state. Florida went from a tropical wilderness to a tropical paradise, for those affluent enough to afford it. Historic menus from the Gilded Age, which showcase lavish meals served at luxury hotels and tattered menus from roadside diners, reflect the culinary changes of an emerging population. Gone were the ox-carts, covered wagons and stagecoaches. Instead, railroads and steamboats brought a new era to the Sunshine State, with pathways to and throughout Florida. Towns, resorts and industries grew at a rapid pace, changing the dining habits of Floridians once again.

The first hotel in Florida was the Ximenez-Fatio boardinghouse in Saint Augustine. Today, it houses a museum, but long before resort hotels dotted the coastline, it opened as a general store and tavern in 1798, run by the Ximenez family. In the 1830s, it was enlarged and served as boardinghouse owned and operated by Louisa Fatio in the mid-1800s. In a detached coquina kitchen, a wood-burning cylindrical beehive oven was used to bake pies, cakes and coontie bread. Meals were served family-style with a variety of dishes utilizing the natural resources in the area such as turkey, bear, deer, seafood, sea turtles, beef, fruits and vegetables.

Before rail travel became popular, steam-powered boats on the rivers and waterways brought tourists, travelers and supplies to hotels along the way. Popular hotels in the late 1800s were the Saint James Hotel, in Jacksonville, and the Coconut Grove House, in Palm Beach. The Coconut Grove House

The Ximenez-Fatio House Museum in Saint Augustine was a general store, a tavern and a nineteenth-century boardinghouse; today, it is a lifestyle museum.

Opposite: An 1888 dinner menu from Flagler's Hotel Ponce de Leon in Saint Augustine. Today, the hotel is a part of Flagler College.

was originally built as a home but was later expanded as an inn where hotel guests dined on fish, green turtle, venison and vegetables. Barbour mentions dining at the Titus Hotel, in Brevard County, along the Indian River, where he was served oysters, clams, fish, shark-steaks, turtle-steaks, tropical fruits and vegetables. Other hotels along waterways made arrangements for guests to go on hunting and fishing excursions. Guests were allowed to pick their own vegetables or shoot waterfowl from the veranda or fish out of the window and have the catch cooked to their liking.

Englishman F. Trench Townshend traveled throughout the state in 1875 and recounted, in his book *Wild Life in Florida: With a Visit to Cuba*, his first taste of "cabbage" from the cabbage palm on the shores of Lake Myakka. Venison, pork, salt-beef and fish were offered in Punta Russa, and turtle soup and steak were offered in the Keys. His usual midday meal consisted of coffee, fried bacon, hominy and biscuits, so the extremely juicy Indian

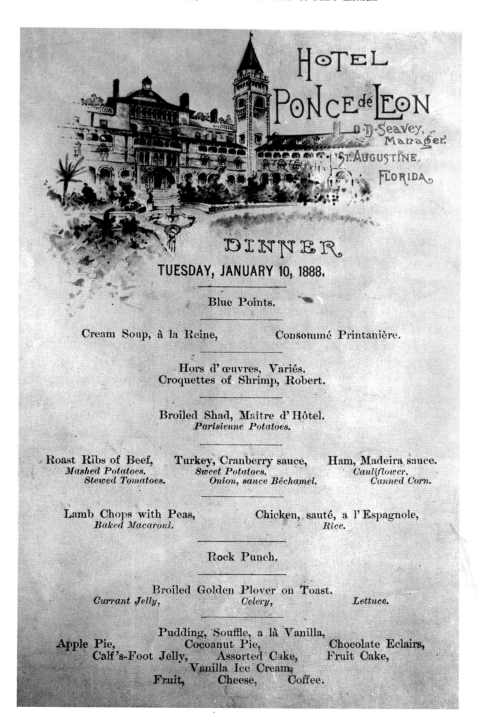

HOTEL PONCE de LEON

O.D.Seavey, Manager.

St.Augustine, Florida.

DINNER

TUESDAY, JANUARY 10, 1888.

Blue Points.

Cream Soup, à la Reine,   Consommé Printanière.

Hors d'œuvres, Variés.
Croquettes of Shrimp, Robert.

Broiled Shad, Maître d'Hôtel.
Parisienne Potatoes.

Roast Ribs of Beef,   Turkey, Cranberry sauce,   Ham, Madeira sauce.
Mashed Potatoes.   *Sweet Potatoes.*   *Cauliflower.*
Stewed Tomatoes.   *Onion, sauce Béchamel.*   *Canned Corn.*

Lamb Chops with Peas,   Chicken, sauté, a l'Espagnole,
Baked Macaroni.   *Rice.*

Rock Punch.

Broiled Golden Plover on Toast.
Currant Jelly,   *Celery,*   *Lettuce.*

Pudding, Souffle, a là Vanilla,
Apple Pie,   Cocoanut Pie,   Chocolate Eclairs,
Calf's-Foot Jelly,   Assorted Cake,   Fruit Cake,
Vanilla Ice Cream,
Fruit,   Cheese,   Coffee.

Boating was a popular pastime for visitors throughout the Sunshine State, as shown here on the pier at Pass-a-Grille.

River oranges, of which he ate many, were a welcome treat. Spurred by detailed descriptions of Florida by writers like Barbour and Townshend, more people made their way to the state. Pensacola, Jacksonville, Tampa and Key West were important harbor cities, and the golden age of steamers continued until the railroad made its way into the interior and southern parts of the state. The coastline and interior grew as a result of the improved transportation system. Steamboat tours were trendy with tourists, and dining onboard offered a variety of seafood, as well as wines and desserts. Palatka was a popular stop for the steamboat and railway lines crossing the state. The steamboat *Madison*, on the Suwannee, served as a country store as well as a mode of transportation, bringing beef, chickens, eggs, hogs and honey to the people of the area. The lower deck of these boats held the cargo and mail, while the upper deck was reserved for passengers.

The Koreshan Unity Settlement, a religious group, chose Estero, in southwest Florida, to set up a utopia in 1894. They built a general store and bakery, serving over five hundred loaves of bread a day, and were famous for making "risin' bread." Orchards and the vegetable garden produced enough to sustain a restaurant on the property. With steamboats serving as a general store for many along the waterways, the Koreshan store was a popular spot for locals and travelers.

Clyde Steamship Company

ST. JOHNS RIVER LINES

W. H. CARLTON, Captain

W. H. BIGGS, Mate   C. K. COOPER, Purser

THOMAS WASHINGTON, Pilot   N. WOODS, Pilot

C. W. LANSING, Chief Engineer   J. W. HOFFMAN, Asst. Engineer

W. J. LEACH, Steward

Merry Christmas Dinner

Indian Relish

Chicken Consomme Royal

Celery   Olives   Pickled Peaches

Broiled Fresh Water Bass, Drawn Butter

Fruit Fritters, Vanilla Sauce

Macaroni au Gratin

Stuffed Vermont Turkey, Cranberry Jelly

Roast Fresh Ham, Candied Yams

Roast Prime of Ribs of Beef, au Jus

Mashed Potatoes   Green Peas

Steamed Rice   Asparagus Tips

Waldorf Salad

Mince Pie   Pumpkin Pie

Ice Cream   Assorted Cakes

Fruit   Nuts   Raisins

Fruit Cake

Cheese   Crackers

Demi-Tasse

S. S. City of Jacksonville

Clyde River Line

A menu from the Clyde Steamship Company's steamboat the SS *City of Jacksonville* featured a Christmas Special in 1926.

Rail service grew and improved throughout the 1880s. Henry Bradley Plant brought steamships and rail lines to Tampa, and in 1884, the Western Railway Company celebrated the completion of a line from Savannah to Gainesville with a dinner of roast beef, mutton, corned beef, ham, veal, venison, dried beef, wild turkey, chicken, duck, shrimp, clams, lobsters, lettuce, cucumbers, Bermuda onions, radishes, celery and tomatoes. Railroad construction continued as Henry Flagler completed the East Coast Railway to the Florida Keys. Cedar Key was the Gulf terminus of the Florida Transit Railway, traveling from Fernandina in northeast Florida. Hundreds of miles of rail had been built to replace the crude roads and trails, and steamship routes linked up with the railroads for international travel from Florida. Later, air-rail service would be offered, for a short time, from New York to Miami via trains and on to points in the Caribbean from there. By the end of the nineteenth century, a modern Florida was emerging, and the Gilded Age helped put the state on the map as the "American Riviera." These were exciting times in the transportation industry as Anthony "Tony" Jannus made the first commercial flight in the world from Saint Petersburg to Tampa on January 1, 1914.

Luxury homes and resorts were designed for travelers to stay for months at a time along with their servants, maids and nannies. At the turn of the twentieth century, two of Florida's first luxury resorts were Plant's Tampa Bay Hotel, with its sparkling minarets, and Flagler's Breakers, in Palm Beach. Plant and Flagler established a chain of resorts, Flagler on the East Cost and Plant inland and along the Gulf Coast. Flagler's Hotel Ponce de Léon was his first in Florida, and Plant's Tampa Bay Hotel featured a reading room and a basement bar, or rathskeller, for men. For women, there were parlors and tearooms. There were separate dining areas for children, cafés and grills, and formal dining rooms served exotic local fare. Telephones, electric lights, indoor plumbing, electric trolleys and bicycles were introduced.

Private, posh Pullman cars offered luxurious accommodations for the affluent, and by the 1900s, the passenger trains carried names such as the Flamingo and Orange Blossom Special. Dining on the train required special preparation for the five-course meals, and tables were set with flowers, tablecloths, fine linens and china. The two Henrys, Flagler and Plant, brought together major population centers with their railroads. Others, like William Chipley, built railroads in the Panhandle, which enabled goods to be shipped from the Pensacola port to areas across the state, including mail-order goods such as cookware and seeds. Cattle, citrus and other agricultural products were more easily shipped to other parts of the state

Henry Plant's Tampa Bay Hotel lit up the sky on opening night with electric lights ablaze in 1891. Also known as "Plant's Palace," the hotel hosted fancy balls, tea parties and a variety of excursions and activities for the guests who wintered there.

and country with these new rail lines. Railroad building led to town building, with accommodations for workers and visitors. Boardinghouses were built, along with logging mills and sawmills, which worked twenty-four hours a day. Vegetable farmers started increasing their acreage to match demand. Thanks to the two Henrys, the state of Florida was transformed into a magical vacation wonderland with fairy tale–like surroundings.

While transporting construction supplies and mail-order goods, crews cooked on board using a skillet or Dutch oven and a coal stove, preparing a breakfast of bacon, eggs, potatoes and brewed coffee; for dinner, ham, baked beans and Mulligan stew were popular choices. Railroads brought new foods to rural areas, but it was the refrigerated rail car that had a significant impact on the foodways of Florida. Before John Gorrie developed a process for artificial refrigeration, ice, from locations like Wenham Lake in Massachusetts, was an important source for keeping foods cold. Ice was harvested, packed in sawdust and transported by ship around the world. Rail cars shipping produce from Florida to Chicago or New York were packed in a type of portable ice, but unlike today, passenger trains took precedence over freight trains, and the ice melted. Years after Gorrie's discovery, refrigerated rail cars became more dependable, and the national distribution of food began with

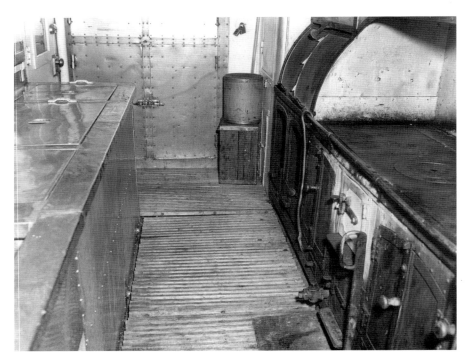

The kitchens of the dining cars on the trains that ran through Florida in the mid-1900s were not so glamorous, such as this one of the Atlantic Coast Line Railway Company.

the completion of the transcontinental railroad. By the 1880s, refrigerated railcars were bringing a variety of foods from across the country to and from the Sunshine State, changing the diet and dining table of Floridians since food no longer had to be consumed near the source.

The early 1900s brought the automobile, and the ease of traveling through the state by car brought more tourists. As cars became more affordable, more people came to vacation and, in turn, to stay in the state. They came in Model T's, and the "Tin Can Tourists" fished in lakes and streams to supplement their dinner from a can. Hotels, resorts and restaurants were expensive, so they stayed in their cars. Auto-camps, cabins, cottages and small motor courts were often located near a general store and filling station for supplies. Some camps provided a dry place to sleep in a studio-like apartment with a community shower building located in the center of camp and a small store that sold essentials for an overnight stay.

The antecedent of tourism in Florida was the establishment of transportation routes for early commercial agriculture and the cattle

Decorative labels on crates of produce shipped north were designed to entice visitors to come to the Sunshine State.

and citrus industries, allowing products to be shipped north in less than a week. Once-popular vacation destinations like Saint Augustine and Pensacola experienced decline as these same routes opened up the state to the south. Mom-and-pop hotels and industries were appearing along this transportation network that carried food and tourists. Remote areas became major agriculture producers as truck farmers started shipping their produce to markets up north. Train conductors warned them about frost to come with four long blasts from the train whistle, giving the farmers time to protect their crops by covering them or lighting smudge pots in the groves.

The same temperate-to-tropical temperature that welcomed tourists also provided an environment for growing citrus, berries and other produce. When Barbour traveled through the area, he noted the abundance of "orange, lemon, fig, guava, garden vegetables, cane, rice, wheat, corn and livestock…green peas, tomatoes, beans, cucumber, onions, cabbages, cauliflower, spinach, celery, lettuce, beets and watermelon …(with) strawberries rapidly becoming a leading crop." Florida products have long been recognized by their geographical region: Key limes, Zellwood corn, Ruskin tomatoes, Plant City strawberries and Indian River citrus. Tupelo honey from northern Florida and mangrove honey from Central Florida are only pieces of the honey production in the state. Tropical fruits from southern Florida complement the peanuts and watermelons across the Panhandle.

The cattle industry has long been an integral part of Florida's heartland, alongside the rolling hills and fenced-in horse farms. It started when Juan Ponce de Léon and other European explorers brought cattle, horses and dogs to the state. In 1637, "La Chula," today's Paynes Prairie, was the original location of the Spanish colonial ranches and the origin of Florida's—and by extension, America's—cattle industry. Cattle and wild horses seen on the prairie today are descendants of those turned loose by the Spanish in the early 1500s. For years, Florida was an open-range state, where the cattle roamed freely and former slaves showed Indian chiefs how to round up herds. Spring cattle roundups drove the herds to ports for shipping. Cracker cow pens were scattered across the state, usually about a day apart, and a roundup could take weeks to months. In Florida, cow handlers are referred to as cowmen, not cowboys, but are also often called Crackers. One way to explain the origin of the name "Cracker" is the use of a long ten- to twelve-foot whip, made of braided leather, that popped with a loud crack when used.

An article in *Harper's* magazine featured "Cracker Cowboys of Florida," but Crackers will quickly tell you they are cowmen, not cowboys.

Each cowman was responsible for his own food. This excerpt from *Biscuits and 'Taters*, by Joe G. Warner, sums up dinner time: "Before the roundup...women would bake dozens of biscuits and sweet potatoes...pack those with a slab of salt bacon, coffee and sometimes an onion for dessert." A fire was started to boil the coffee, and a slab of bacon was "put on a palmetto stalk and broiled over the fire...if water was scarce, salt on the boiling bacon was washed off in the coffee...Greasy salty coffee was good...ate taters first, scraped mold off the hardened biscuits and toasted them. On extended drives, the meat and sausage were fried and then packed into five-gallon tins and then fat poured over it in order for the meat to keep." Often grits and corn pone were a part of this campfire meal. An 1876 living-history cow camp at Lake Kissimmee State Park re-creates what life was like at the time. The town of Kissimmee, once known as "Cow Town," had a ride-in bar for those not wanting to get off their horses after a hard day's work. In the 1930s, the Florida Cattleman's Association and the Florida Citrus Commission were created.

Europeans built massive, elaborate, ornate greenhouses, called orangeries, for the cultivation of citrus and protection from the cold. The Sunshine State is a natural home to citrus production, and we can thank the Europeans for introducing citrus to the state in the sixteenth century with the arrival of explorers from Italy and Spain and the seeds they planted or dropped during their explorations. Spanish law required sailors to carry seeds with them when traveling to the New World. The sandy soil and subtropical climate was ideal, and by the 1800s, wild orange groves could be found throughout many of Florida's forests and along the Saint Johns River. Today, many citrus products are produced by a co-op of Florida citrus growers, such as Florida's Natural Growers in Lake Wales. The Grove House visitors' center features an educational center that showcases the growing, processing and packaging of citrus, from grove to glass. The horticulture exhibit shows the growing cycle of citrus from seed to harvest. Oranges are processed into juice within twenty-four hours of picking, and the spent peels and pulp are turned into cattle feed. From planting and raising the trees to processing and packaging the product, the growers pride themselves on bringing quality juice to the market. With over 500,000 acres of citrus groves throughout Florida, the cooperative includes 50,000 acres and over one thousand growers. It is the largest grower and distributor of citrus and juice products in the United States. Florida is credited with the development of the modern grapefruit, descendant of the pomelo. The French count Odet Philippe introduced grapefruit when he planted the first grove near Tampa in 1823. The orange blossom is the state

A welcome center in Marianna featured orange juice and maps for travelers to Florida. This photograph was taken in 1954.

flower and orange juice the state beverage, so it's only natural that Florida welcome stations have been serving it up since the 1950s.

With a coastline stretching over one thousand miles and hundreds of species swimming in the waters, the bounty in Florida's waters has provided a source of nutrition for thousands of years. Fishing was and is an integral part of what makes up Florida foodways. Commercial fishing was launched in Florida with fishing ranchos from Jupiter Inlet south to the Florida Keys and up the Gulf Coast to Tampa Bay, where fish was packed, dried and shipped. Salted preservation preceded ice and cold storage. Fish were split and pressed to remove juices, then rubbed with salt to aid in extracting moisture, before being packed for shipment. The fish would be good for a year and made a convenient protein source for inland Crackers. Although fishing is the oldest industry in Florida, with today's commercial bans and catch limits, the offerings are on a limited seasonal basis. The Florida Maritime Museum, in Cortez, and the Sebastian Fishing Museum, on the eastern coast, offer a glimpse into the life of early commercial fishermen. Florida is synonymous with seafood, as each region captures a taste of the state. With Apalachicola oysters, Steinhatchee scallops, Florida Keys spiny lobster, Cedar Keys stone crab, Cortez mullet, Crystal River blue crab and Fernandina shrimp, the list is almost as endless as the towns, and the seafood is not limited to a specific region. Aquaculture is the fastest-growing segment of world food production, necessary to supplement the demand for Florida's wild seafood.

From the emerald-green waters of Perdido Key to the southernmost point in Key West, you are never far from the Atlantic Ocean or Gulf of Mexico. To grasp the geographical diversity, spanning from the most pristine beaches and hilly canopy roads of Tallahassee, heading south across open prairies, passing from temperate to tropical to the southernmost point and shell-paved streets of the Keys, one must visit each region to truly capture a taste of Florida. From the Casa Monica hotel in Saint Augustine to the Casa Marina in Key West, the lodging throughout the state not only reflects unique architectural styles but is also a regional reflection of the local menu. In 1576, the Olmos family of Saint Augustine opened the first restaurant and tavern in the United States, but one of the oldest continuously operating restaurants in Florida is Staff's Restaurant, in Fort Walton Beach. Opened in 1913 at the former Gulfview Hotel, diners ate in the owners' personal dining room. The restaurant was so popular it had to be moved in 1931 into a converted garage on the property. The Columbia Café, founded in 1905 in Ybor City by Cuban immigrant Casimiro Hernandez Sr., morphed into the Columbia Restaurant chain, famous for its award-winning 1905 Salad. Now on the National Register of Historic Places, it started out as a sixty-seat corner café. It has the distinction of being the oldest restaurant still open in all of Florida.

As tourism increased, so did dining options. Duncan Hines developed the first restaurant guide, featuring many Florida restaurants, including the Columbia Café. Initially, he and his wife wrote the guide for friends, but the request for more information continued so, by 1938, he published the fifth edition of *Adventures in Good Eating: A Directory of Good Eating Places Along the Highways and in Villages and Cities of America.* Motorists traveling to the state with the luxury of a personal automobile wanted to enjoy the regional cuisine. Major roadways were dotted with restaurants and motels offering reasonable rates. Hines gave brief descriptions to accompany many of the listings.

At the Brevard Hotel in Cocoa, "cooking is done exclusively by electricity, the Brevard having one of the few kitchens so equipped in the state." At the Garden Grill in Daytona Beach, "individual 'hot pot' luncheons are featured." At Christine's at Eau Gallie, Hines suggests stopping by the Jelly

Kitchen and picking up some guava jelly and marmalade. The Log Cabin Tea Room in West Palm Beach was serving fried chicken and waffles at the time. At the Palm Tea Room in Miami Beach, the specialty was liver and bacon, served three times a day. Some of these places are still open today, such as the Lakeside Inn in Mount Dora, where fresh vegetables and fruits were guaranteed to be on the menu. Joe's Place in Miami Beach opened over one hundred years ago and then, around 1921, began serving stone crab. Joe's Stone Crab is still serving the claws.

Chalet Suzanne of Lake Wales received the most attention from Hines, with a lengthy description promoting the area as well. "The Bok Singing Tower and Cypress Gardens are only a ten-minute ride from this beautiful chalet, which is a rambling structure set in the midst of 230 rolling acres of orange trees and lily pools near the shore of Lake Suzanne." The chalet also had a soup cannery, where Carl Hinshaw created his now-famous romaine soup (also known as moon soup) after a trip to the moon on *Apollo 15*. According to the National Register of Historic Places, the soup cannery opened in 1956. Sadly, the Chalet Suzanne closed on August 4, 2014.

The Putnam Lodge made the list, only stating the location was in Shamrock. The Putnam Lumber Company originally built the lodge, along with an ice plant and dairy, for the community. New owners, Ed and Beverly Pivacek, carefully restored and renovated the Putman Lodge Hotel and Spa, just north of Cross City on Old Dixie Highway. Reopened in 2014, the dining room today looks as if you have stepped back in time to when the Putnam Lodge first opened in 1927. The Garden Seat in Clearwater served lunch and dinner on a screened porch overlooking the bay, and tea was served in the garden. Hines must have been impressed, since he featured a photo and stated, "I doubt if more delicious food is served in Florida." No liquor was served at that time, but later "The Pub" became a part of Siple's Garden Seat, as mentioned in another restaurant guide aimed at motorists, *The New Ford Treasury of Favorite Recipes from Famous Restaurants*. Another Florida restaurant listed in the Ford book that is still open is The Grill in Apalachicola. Opened in 1903, a recipe for its hush puppies and a mention of the Gorrie Museum is included in the description. The Rod and Gun Club, once a part of a Seminole trading post and today a historic landmark in Everglades City, still serves lunch and dinner. The original *Ford Treasury of Recipes from Famous Eating Places* from the 1950s also includes the Columbia Restaurant and Chalet Suzanne.

After the turn of the twentieth century, the San Carlos Hotel in Pensacola served a special Thanksgiving dinner, and resort hotels catered to a new

Today, the newly reopened Putnam Lodge dining room looks much the same as it does in this early photo.

group of tourists during the boom era of the state. The Vinoy Hotel of Saint Petersburg and the Don CeSar on Saint Pete Beach, dubbed the "Pink Lady," were open only in the winter. The Colony Hotel and Cabana Club at Delray Beach provided vibrant nightlife and featured sea grapes on the menu. The Brazilian Court Hotel and Beach Club of Palm Beach became a favorite tourist spot, as did the Biltmore in Coral Gables. Soon Miami Beach became "America's Winter Playground."

9

Eternal Vacation in the Sunshine State

Northern Florida is possibly as different from an outsider's perceptions of Florida as can be. Caverns and waterfalls are found in what are now designated state parks. Along the western coast, rolling hills, bluffs and pine forests complement the snow-white Appalachian quartz sand and gem-colored sparkling waters of the Gulf of Mexico. On the eastern coast, the Gulf Stream waves lap ashore the cream-colored sandy beaches of the Atlantic Ocean. Mild summers ultimately give way to cold, sometimes icy, winters, as this temperate region experiences a "cold snap" on occasion.

The variety and quantity of seafood helped the area around Pensacola earn the title "Red Snapper Capital of the World" in 1868, while my hometown, Panama City, is home to the "World's Most Beautiful Beaches." Pensacola, the "City of Five Flags," is known for its Spanish and Creole cooking, and the Seville Square historic district of the old city area reflects the past and present with old wrought-iron balconies. New restaurants replace the once-common gopher tortoise dishes with other locally sourced foods.

Unique events such as the annual Wausau Possum Festival and the Flora-Bama Lounge, Package and Oyster Bar "Mullet Toss" on Perdido Key are complemented by the tupelo honey for sale along the backwoods roads near the "Forgotten Coast." Bars such as Outzs Too, near Wakulla Springs, which spring out of nowhere along the route, offer fresh oysters from Florida's oyster capital, Apalachicola. Apalachicola oysters are just as popular at fish camps as they are at five-star restaurants. These succulent bivalves are the

Oystermen have been using the same long-handled tongs to pull up oysters onto their boats for over a century, as shown on this oyster boat at the dock on Apalachicola Bay in the late 1800s.

result of just the right temperature in the brackish water created when the river meets the gulf at Apalachicola Bay.

Old Florida towns are sprinkled around the state, in places like Everglades City and Clewiston to the south, Cedar Key and Steinhatchee along the western coast and DeFuniak Springs to the north, while northwest Florida's Gulf Coast shores are home to burgeoning seaside communities. All rely on the same ingredients to keep tourists coming back: the rich natural resources from freshwater fishing, quail and deer hunting or combing the area for figs, persimmons and pears for a taste of old Florida. At one time, regional cooking in North Florida was a reflection of the Old South, when wild hogs still roamed the sand dunes. Today, North Florida shares an Alabama-Georgia boundary and is as southern as sweet tea in the antebellum towns of Madison, Monticello, Quincy and Marianna. Watermelons, with seed-spitting contests on the front lawn; country-fried steak; "smothered" quail or chicken; fried catfish; and freshly sliced garden tomatoes are still a part of the essence of North Florida. Certain dishes can be found on many menus across the area, like fried mullet, grouper, catfish, hush puppies, coleslaw, cheese grits and, of course, sweet tea. Driving the two-lane roads along the tranquil Forgotten Coast, dotted with rural communities and myriad restaurants, is an unforgettable sojourn. Inland, the state capital, Tallahassee, is home to emerging restaurants and home cooks preparing the traditional foods of the area. "The Original Recipe for Hushpuppies," from O.P. Shields of Saint Marks, is featured in *Camellia Cookery* from 1950s. Junior Service Leagues continue to preserve the past by creating cookbooks such as Panama City's *Bay Leaves* and the fifty-year-old, ever-popular *Gasparilla Cookbook* from Tampa.

Traveling east across the state, there are more regional favorites, such as Datil peppers and pink shrimp from the Saint Augustine area. At one time, the Jacksonville area grew more eggplant than any other part of the nation. Fernandina Beach, on Amelia Island, boasts a history of flying more flags than any other city in the nation and is home to Florida's oldest tavern, the Palace Saloon, which opened in 1878. Fernandina Beach, on the Atlantic, was once connected by Florida's first cross-state rail to secluded Cedar Key, on the Gulf of Mexico. Both are still thriving spots for tourists and locals to enjoy a variety of old and new dining experiences.

By the 1950s, automobiles, mosquito control and air conditioning opened up Florida to the rest of the nation. Federal laws mandated working hours, so vacations become a standard part of the American dream, with trips to the Singing Tower, at Bok Gardens, and Silver Springs. Later, Cypress Gardens and Weeki Wachee Springs became popular destinations. Going beyond the world-renowned beaches and theme parks, the middle of the state is now notable for its cruise ports and famous Space Port. Space ice cream, found in many Florida gift shops, is a unique treat. Today, the Florida Aquarium, Disney World, Universal Studios and Busch Gardens theme parks help make Florida the vacation wonderland it is. Epcot World Showcase introduces even more new foods and cultures to an already culturally diverse state.

Hidden among the rich estuaries and coastal waters of the central Gulf Coast area is Weedon Island. This archaeological jewel also housed a popular speakeasy during Prohibition that became a 1930s movie studio and later the Grand Central Airport, with the national hub for Eastern Air Transport, later known as Eastern Airlines. With its rich history, the Tampa Bay area is home to some of the most diverse dining options in the state. Tarpon Springs was known first as the "Venice of the South" in the late 1800s, with its winding waterway and Victorian-style mansions. Later, the

"Sponge Capital of the World" brought Greek sponge divers and their families to Tarpon Springs, and they built a community that reflects their rich heritage. Popular dishes such as pastittsio, moussaka, spanakopita and baklava are found in local homes and restaurants.

In 1885, Don Vicente Martinez Ybor from Cuba, along with a Spanish civil engineer from New York, came to the area looking for guavas but, instead, set up what was to become the "Cigar Capital of the World." Cuban and Spanish cigar makers lived in *casitas*, small wooden-frame houses, in Ybor City. They drew water from an outside well before heating it up on the stove to make *café con leche*. To go with the coffee, for three cents a loaf, cuban bread was delivered each morning. Impaled on a nail at the front door, this crusty-on-the-outside, soft-on-the-inside bread is enjoyed today at homes and restaurants throughout the Tampa Bay area. Cuban sandwiches and deviled crabs were created in Ybor City, using the bread for the sandwich and the stale breadcrumbs for the deviled crab.

Celery production in Sarasota and cucumber production in Wauchula were once as common as poultry and egg production was in Masaryktown. The early Czechoslovakian population of the area turned from citrus to chicken farming, after freezing temperatures wiped out the groves. They found enough success to be dubbed, in 1956, the "Egg Capital of Florida."

Today, the village of Cortez, located on Sarasota Bay, is one of the few remaining active commercial fishing waterfronts in Florida, with generations of fishermen and -women working the area. Fishing ranchos established by the Spanish were later home to commercial fishermen of English descent. The area south of the village was referred to as "the kitchen," as its wealth of seafood made it possible for them to feed their families. Net fishing for the huge schools of black mullet was the core of the Cortez fishing industry, and thousands of pounds were caught annually, processed and shipped to Cedar Key or Tampa for distribution. Today, mullet roe, also called "Florida caviar," is a part of the industry.

Heading south, the Orange Blossom Special took vacationers to West Palm Beach, with routes traversing the peninsula and showing off the natural beauty of the state. An increase in affordable automobiles and new roadways, such as the Tamiami Trail, encouraged travel across the southern part of the Sunshine State. Palm Beach is known for its ritzy shopping districts and fancy hotels, but the pineapple belt once skirted the area, before Flagler built his luxury resorts. Early settlers found a vast supply of coconuts from shipwrecks' cargo and planted the trees that fill the area today. Saint Lucie County to the north was known as the

The Orange Blossom Special popularized train travel throughout tropical Florida.

"Pineapple Capital of the World," but the pineapple belt stretched west across the state, along the Caloosahatchee River and south to Miami. South Florida continued to grow and expand culturally as well, with an influx of Cubans following the 1959 revolution.

Today, traveling across the state from Tampa to Miami by train gives a glimpse of backyard gardens, rows of corn stalks, barbecue pits, white sands, cows and orange groves, both thriving and abandoned. When you reach South Florida, along the Atlantic Coast, and the explosion that is Miami, the rollicking beats and crashing waves along the shore at South Beach exemplify the average American's perception of Florida. Its tropical summers; flat wetlands; sprawled out, mid-century suburban communities; and Art Deco hotels are the true stereotype. The landscape is covered in shopping malls and highways, between renowned beaches.

Long after the Tequesta traveled the local waterways, the village of Miami was established in the late 1890s, and soon the Miccosukee and Seminole made way for Henry Flagler, who brought a new crop of travelers. This tropical region soon became known for its sugarcane, bananas and other produce, such as avocados (alligator pear), mangoes, grapefruit, Key limes, cucumbers, tomatoes, eggplant, peppers and beans.

In the 1920s, Miami Beach's burgeoning Jewish culture introduced latkes, stuffed cabbage, chopped chicken livers, matzo balls and bagels to the area. Miami today is a melting pot with "Little Havana" at the center of the Cuban culture. You will find ample essentials to produce some of the best Cuban cuisine in the state with plantains, cassava and *boniatos* (sweet potatoes). The southernmost point in the state, Key West, home of the Conch Republic, feels like a Caribbean island. Pan American World Airways, also known as Pan Am, was founded in Key West in 1927, for carrying mail and passengers. From the urban oasis of Miami and South Beach to the slower-paced islands of Captiva and Sanibel to the west, South Florida is a tropical paradise.

Tropical fruits provide a taste of Florida sunshine, but the pretty-pink-on-the-inside and green-on-the-outside guava has so many seeds it is difficult to eat fresh, so the paste is popular. Thick enough to slice and eat, this sweet paste is often served with cream cheese and saltines or made into popovers with a guava–cream cheese filling. In the late 1800s, George M. Barbour traveled across the state and explained the acquired taste of the guava: "It's like eating a strawberry inside of an orange." The Palmetto Canning Company started producing guava jelly in 1927 and, at one time, sea grape preserves as well. The star-shaped carambola is as unique in its flavor as its shape. When sliced cross-wise, it makes a great garnish or snack. Mango and papaya smoothies are only a couple of the choices available. Loquats and kumquats are not only tropical treats, they are also found integrated into the landscape of the state.

Along the southwest shore of the state, cocquina was once canned and sold as "Ko-Kee-Na" in Fort Myers. A broth made from the plentiful coquina in the area was produced in large quantities there. A simple, quick, homemade soup of well-rinsed shells, simmered until they pop open, creates a taste somewhat like clam broth. The myriad of tiny bivalves burrowing in the sand along the shore help to make a game of plucking up handfuls of them as the waves recede, before they come crashing down upon the wet, sponge-like sand. Clam canning factories of quahog and littlenecks were set up on Marco Island, where they were steamed and packed for shipment in the early 1900s.

Florida was a land of promise, and hand-powered ice cream makers and butter churners were to become nostalgic reminders of the past. The nineteenth century introduced the refrigerator, at first called an icebox, and later a compartmentalized refrigerator-freezer. The gas range with automatic pilot lights appeared in Florida kitchens around the 1930s. Elements of both were combined to create a dessert, called Alaska-Florida, to commemorate the United States' purchase of Alaska; the name was later changed to baked Alaska. The dish has a warm, golden-brown egg white topping and a frozen ice cream center. It's often served as a grand finale on cruise ships returning to port. Laborsaving devices and economical manufactured goods, electricity and new forms of communication, such as the telegraph, telephone and typewriter, were welcomed in homes across the state. Railroads and mail-order catalogues were changing the way Floridians procured and cooked their foods. Door-to-door peddlers delivering goods in horse-drawn wagons were replaced by grocery stores carrying name-brand and pre-packaged foods.

Grocery stores made cooking at home easier than ever. In 1916, the first self-service grocery store opened in Memphis, named Piggly Wiggly. Someone in North Florida liked it so well he opened his own Hoggly Woggly, and the Jitney Jungle opened in 1927. The first Florida grocery store chain, Publix Food Stores, opened in Winter Haven in 1930. In the 1940s, Publix Super Market opened with terrazzo floors and air conditioning, providing a truly modern marketplace. Refrigerated rail cars and improved canning techniques competed with truck farmers selling local produce. As regional markets grew, national products became common, and the use of these convenience foods was the standard for quality home dining.

Universities were created in Tallahassee and Gainesville, teaching men and boys new farming techniques, and female teachers offered classes on cooking and home food canning to women and girls. It was Ellen Richards, an MIT chemist in the late 1880s, who did the most to change the face of the American kitchen. Using her scientific knowledge, she wrote *The Chemistry of Cooking and Cleaning: Manual for Housekeepers* and created the American Home Economics Association (AHEA) in order to improve living conditions in the home and community. Home economists became pioneers in developing timesaving ways to get women out of the kitchen and into the workforce. Around that same time, Fannie Farmer published *The Boston Cooking-School Cook Book*, which had precise measurements. The advent of gas stoves also allowed for better temperature control. The Cooperative Extension Services provided a link between new research and development at land-grant colleges, and county agents visited homes and farms, sharing ideas for better ways to prepare, preserve and even market food.

The Florida frontier did not officially shut down until the mid-century, when the open range was penned in by a 1949 law requiring fences in order to reduce bovine accidents on the newly paved highway system. Historic Florida main streets today reflect this time period with a sense of nostalgia for the "good old days," with century-old homes, sidewalks, diners, family-

The 1940s home demonstration club of Falling Creek, in Columbia County, uses a pressure cooker for this canning demonstration.

owned restaurants, general stores and docks for fishing. Leading up to World War II, the Great Depression followed this idyllic era in Florida. Victory gardens were encouraged and planted, while county extension agents and home economists provided guidance during the wartime shortages, including recipes for preparing healthful meals with limited means. In 1941,

In 1942 during World War II, students at the Florida State College for Women in Tallahassee worked in the College Defense Garden.

resort hotels were converted to housing or hospitals for our soldiers, sailors and aviators. Rationing boards were created to deal with limited supplies of sugar, coffee, meats and butter on the homefront.

Home economics became a central part of public school education. Jell-O, miniature marshmallows, canned vegetables, soups and cake mixes filled kitchen cupboards. Instant ingredients like grits, potatoes, oatmeal, coffee, pudding, milk and refrigerated canned biscuits graced many dining tables. These convenience foods at home would soon be replaced with fast food. Electric ranges and electric skillets, along with deep-fat fryers, were replacing the cast-iron cookware of our mothers and grandmothers. Congress passed the School Lunch Act in 1946, but it was once again MIT chemist and home economist Ellen Richards who started the first school lunch program in Boston, years earlier. A Pinellas County health official began the process long before laws were passed. In 1914, he put a big white cow in the playground and offered every child a half pint of milk. Later, mothers and the school principal worked together to give the children a bowl of soup each day, along with vegetables from the school garden.

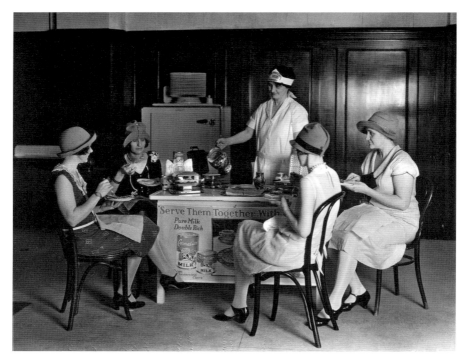

Cooking demonstrations with commercially canned products were one way to introduce and promote brand names, such as the one shown here in 1927 for Carnation milk.

A collection of papers from the Florida Heritage Collection tells *The School Lunch Story* (also the title of the work) from 1958. As experienced by our prehistoric ancestors, "feast and famine" was a concern. For example, the 1956–57 school year was bountiful with commodities, but the following year found cafeterias in short supply due to flu, freeze, flood, fewer commodities and inflation. As a result, Florida pushed for more commodities from local sources to feed its growing children. Peanut butter was made into candy, cookies and cakes and stirred into brownie batter. The addition of commodity cheese improved the flavor of the already delicious yeast rolls and mashed potatoes. A "Festival of Florida Products" was held in school cafeterias to showcase the Florida products used in school lunches around the state and to expose these children to foods they had not previously tasted. Introducing more fruits into the diet; raw, dried, canned and frozen fruit were all encouraged and helped "expand and stabilize Florida farm markets."

The 1950s and 1960s saw the growth of the suburbs, and the cuisine evolved along with food storage and preparation techniques. The mechanized age of refrigeration and freezers gave us more convenience foods. TV dinners were all the rage, offering a complete frozen meal on one disposable foil tray. Restaurant chains were appearing in many towns. From the Depression to the modern era of fine dining and roadside cafés, the food choices grew every day. Home cooks were preparing more variety than ever before as new recipes were being added to traditional holiday menus, such as green bean casserole, Toll House cookies and Rice Krispie treats.

For many, January and New Year's Day begins with the southern traditions of hoppin' john for good luck, ham for good health and collards for wealth. February's strawberries are followed by all things green in March. April is the time to bring out the crystal platter made especially for deviled eggs. May, with Mother's Day dinners and Memorial Day cookouts, is followed closely by more cooking on the grill in June, with Father's Day. The cookout trend comes in handy with hurricane season from June to November, with the occasional loss of electricity. Having charcoal on hand is great when the power goes out and we are right back where the first Floridians started, cooking outdoors. With advanced warning, we have plenty of time to stock up on supplies, especially water, when a storm is approaching. But once it hits, we are back to native-style cooking. Preparing for hurricanes by making and freezing soups and stews that can be heated up on a grill when the power goes out is another way to celebrate the joys of living in the Sunshine State. Soups freeze fairly solidly and act as cooling agents for the cooler. July and August might find you pining for homemade ice cream before September school days are here. By the time fall approaches, the October pumpkin carving and candy-eating season are followed by traditional Thanksgiving, Hanukkah and Christmas dishes. The first Christmas celebrated in Florida was likely when DeSoto and his men camped in what is now Tallahassee. Every month of the year is worth celebrating with Florida favorites.

The 1970s were full of nouvelle cuisine appearing on menus alongside smaller á la carte items, later followed by 1980s steakhouses featuring enormous portions. Access to new foods for all made a dramatic change in the diet of Floridians. Some of the trends remain today, and Florida is home to many national restaurant chains that got their start in the state, such as Burger King, Red Lobster, Outback and Hooters, along with nationally acclaimed restaurants like Bern's Steak House. By the 1990s, detailed cookbooks, on endless subjects, and cooking shows opened the door for cooking channels. Today, cooking competitions, food trucks and festivals are complemented by locally sourced foods and the farm-to-table movement. For nutritious variety and delicious dishes, epicurean delights abound in the Sunshine State.

From the shores of the Atlantic Ocean to the Gulf of Mexico and south to a tropical paradise, the cooking styles today are as varied as the landscape. Indigenous ingredients helped to create menus that reflect not only the environment but the cultural diversity as well. From the highest point in the state, at Lakewood in Walton County, to the Underwater Park of the Florida Keys, places to visit with unique names such as Two Egg, Sopchoppy, Wewahitchka, Howey-in-the-Hills, Weeki Wachee, Pass-a-Grille, Yeehaw Junction, Apopka, Masaryktown, Micanopy, Chokoloskee, Bokeelia, Punta Gorda and Punta Russa to the classic resort towns around the state, living in Florida is like an eternal vacation.

10

ℐ Taste of ℱlorida Sunshine

For thousands of years, Florida was an outdoor supermarket. Early inhabitants gathered herbs and other plants in the wild, caught fish in the many waters and hunted for game throughout the state. The heritage of Florida foods is one of uncompromised diversity across multiple dimensions, and it began long before European explorers reached its shores in the sixteenth century. It started when prehistoric man first migrated to the area and continued to evolve with rapid changes, emerging as industrialized foods were introduced. The state's later culinary history parallels its academic history, and today Florida is the culinary melting pot of the country, with over five hundred years of cultures blending their cooking styles to produce the most diverse and oldest cuisine in America.

The shift in culture and historical cuisine from one end of the state to the other is as varied as its landscape. Today, the Spanish influence is reflected in the regional cuisines of the state, along with Greek, Italian, Minorcan, Cuban, Mexican, French and others. There are also areas in which the natural environment reflects the cuisine, such as Conch and Caribbean cooking in the Keys, Cracker cooking in the heartland and Creole cooking in northwest Florida. Jewish and Seminole influences are also reflected in cooking styles, along with myriad other immigrants who all brought with them cooking techniques to meld with Florida ingredients. As new settlers arrived, their own traditions had as much influence as the natural environment on the foods of the area, creating culinary regions based on material available. Geography, climate, ingredients and tradition all impact the variety of dishes served in homes and restaurants across the peninsula. Over a dozen wineries feature homegrown favorites such as blueberry, muscadine and a variety of citrus wines.

Today, the multicultural essence of food can be found through the senses of taste, sight, texture and smell as we move from the hickory-smoked barbecue to the smell of sizzling olive oil with garlic and other aromatic delights that make up the taste of Florida. Cooking is a way to pass on traditions, and it reflects society at a particular time and location. Recipes are portals to the past that allow us to re-create what our ancestors ate. One way to discover what life might have been like is through recipes and cookbooks dating back to that time period. Using the cooking methods and ingredients of today with the inspiration of the past, the following potpourri of recipes is a tribute to early Floridians.

The Alligator, the Accidental Farmer and the Invasion from Europe

Whether it's over an open pit, around the campfire or on the backyard grill, one can re-create the way the first Floridians cooked by mimicking the style and utilizing the same types of woods for the fire. The Paleo- and Archaic Indians might have learned, through trial and error, that dry, hard wood burns longer and gives a better flavor to the food. Prehistoric cooking can be thought of as pulling weeds and playing with fire, but it takes a trained expert to gather successfully from the wild, so I gathered my ingredients from the market.

Weeds and Fire

The Paleoindian method, with the help of Archaic hickory, is time consuming and somewhat dangerous, but the results will give you a taste unlike traditional grilled meats. By laying the meat directly on hot coals or burying it within the ashes, you can re-create the first cooking method used in the Sunshine State.

Lump charcoal or hickory logs
1 T-bone, ribeye or sirloin steak
4 cups watercress, washed and dried

Place several logs of dried hickory or lump charcoal, not briquettes, in a fire pit or on the bottom grill grate. Burn until ashen and red-hot. This might take a couple hours for wood, less time for charcoal. Carefully fan off the top layer of ash and place the meat directly on the evenly layered burning coals. Turn as necessary to cook until desired doneness. You will probably end up with a Pittsburgh–style steak, rare on the inside and charred on the outside. Brush or blow off ashes before serving on a bed of peppery watercress.

SIZZLE AND DRIZZLE

Steak on a stick was one culinary leap forward for the Archaic Indians. Onions have been growing wild for thousands of years, and when paired with sizzling meat and a little sweet drizzle, the flavor rewards are compounded to create an exciting new taste.

Prickly Pear Drizzle

Florida chefs create new and interesting cuisine from native Florida foods, adding to the state's gastronomic history. The old and the new came together at the JW Marriott Marquis Miami dining room, just around the corner from the Miami circle, a two-thousand-year-old ancient Indian site in downtown Miami. The chef created a dessert using prickly pear, demonstrating that many of the dining options of early man were the same as today, just prepared differently. The sweet-tasting prickly pear, also known as an Indian fig, was a seasonal treat. Native Americans would roll the fruit in grit-like sand or char off the prickly parts in a fire. Removing the spines and glochids can irritate the skin. Wear gloves, even when purchased from the market, to shield your hands from unseen glochids.

4 prickly pears
Honey, to taste
I teaspoon lemon juice

Lightly char the skin by holding the fruit with tongs over an open flame. Wearing gloves, skin the fruit by slicing off both ends and make a long, vertical slice down the body of the pear. Pull or cut away skin. Separate seeds from pulp by pressing through a sieve, catching the juice in a bowl. Alternatively, pulse in a blender until

Pretty and pink, the prickly pear cactus grows wild throughout the state of Florida. *Photographed by Joy Sheffield Harris.*

> liquefied and then strain thorough a fine sieve, mesh strainer or cheesecloth, retaining juice and discarding solids. Boil the strained juice, with honey, to reduce, and stir in a little lemon juice to bring out the flavor. Drizzle the syrup over cooked meat.

Northern tribes relied more on farming and hunting, southern tribes on seafood; both shared their cooking methods with European explorers. Roasting today is defined as a dry-heat cooking method, usually in the oven, but at the time of European exploration, roasting was done in front of or over an open fire. Roasting food by spearing it with a stick and holding it over the fire evolved into the use of the spit and grill. An early method of cooking corn was to roll the husked corn evenly back and forth on the coals of a campfire until caramel-colored. When roasted with the husks removed, the kernels acquire a caramel taste; with the husks in place, it is more like steamed corn. Native Americans commonly used bear fat, but for this recipe, bacon is the choice that provides flavor and aids in browning the turkey legs.

Roasted Turkey Legs and Corn

2 turkey legs, small enough to fit on grill
2 slices bacon
2 ears of corn
Salt and pepper, to taste

Wrap bacon around turkey legs and grill over a medium-low heat for
1½ hours, or until internal temperature reaches 180–185 degrees.
Remove from grill and let stand for 20 minutes while preparing
the corn. Add more charcoal to produce high heat. Trim excess silk
off end of corn and remove outer husks. Turn back inner husks
and remove remaining silks. Replace inner husks and place corn
on grill over medium-low heat. Cook 15–20 minutes, turning
often. Husks will turn brown. (Or you may put the ears, in their
husks, directly on the hot coals and turn every minute or so for
8–10 minutes.) Remove from grill and let cool before removing
remaining husks and serving.

Simple Succotash

*Native Americans provided a foundation for survival to European explorers with the
introduction of new foods, and they also livened up the language with the introduction
of new words such as "succotash," "squash," "opossum," "hickory," "pecan,"
"raccoon" and "hominy," to name a few. The Indian word* succotash *means
"fragments," some of which were meat and sunflower seeds. Colonists added salt pork,
and early settlers added cream, flour and butter to the dish. Crackers used chicken stock
in place of water. By scraping the corn from the cob and simmering the cob in the broth
first, another level of flavor is achieved.*

2 ounces salt pork, cubed
2 cups lima beans, fresh or frozen
½ cup chicken broth
2 cups corn, fresh or frozen
½ cup shredded chicken
2 tablespoons cream
1 teaspoon sugar
Salt and pepper, optional

Fry salt pork over medium-high heat in a large skillet to render the fat. Remove salt pork and add beans; stir to coat them in the fat. Add broth and bring to a boil, reduce heat and simmer 15 minutes. Stir in corn and continue cooking until corn is tender. Remove from heat and stir in chicken, cream and sugar. Season with salt and pepper if desired.

A Thanksgiving soup of garbanzo beans, olive oil, pork and garlic might have been part of the first Thanksgiving celebrated in Florida, long before the Pilgrims broke bread with the Native Americans up the coast. The idea of combining meats and vegetables in a stew to produce something delicious has been carried on for generations. Soups and stews were an economical and easy way to incorporate many of the regional foods in one dish, freeing up time for other chores. At Florida missions, stews were cooked over a fire with the pot attached to a pole, or they used a three-legged iron pot that was placed among the hot coals. Native Americans used herbs and other leaves for flavoring. Culinary herbs enhance the flavor of many dishes, but a couple of those found in the wild are not to be confused with the cooking variety. Florida rosemary, or *Ceratiola ericoides*, is a native of scrub habitats found among the sandhills of North Florida. Also known as false rosemary, it is not *Rosmarinus officinalis*, or culinary rosemary. Florida swamp bay and sweetbay magnolia trees are not the source for culinary bay leaves.

Mission Stew

Combining the foods of two distinctly different cultures—Native American and Spanish, in this case—oftentimes results in the best of both worlds, as this mission stew reveals. Using indigenous ingredients alongside Spanish imports and simmering for hours over an open flame, this stew could be served day or night as desired.

2 tablespoons butter
1 pound beef shank
1 pound pork chop
½ pound chicken breast
1 Spanish onion, chopped
1 clove garlic, minced
1 bay leaf
1 teaspoon salt

½ teaspoon pepper
1 medium butternut squash, peeled, seeded and cut into chunks
1 16-ounce can garbanzo beans, drained
1 cup corn, fresh or frozen
1 cup baby lima beans, frozen
2 tablespoons fine ground cornmeal, optional

In a wide, deep pot, melt butter and then brown beef, pork and chicken on all sides. Stir in onion and garlic; cook 3 minutes. Add 6 cups of water, bay leaf, salt and pepper. Bring to a boil, reduce to a slow simmer and cook covered for 3 hours. Remove bay leaf and bones. (At this point, meat should be falling off the bones.) Increase heat to high, add squash and bring to a boil. Reduce heat to simmer, cover and cook 30–45 minutes, or until squash is tender. Stir in garbanzo beans, corn and lima beans and cook 15 minutes longer. If your stew is too thin, you can stir about 2 tablespoons of fine cornmeal into ¼ cup of water, add to the simmering pot and then continue cooking for 15 minutes.

Fromajardis

A traditional Minorcan Easter pastry seasoned with nutmeg and stuffed with cheese.

Pastry:
1¼ cups flour
½ cup (8 tablespoons) cold butter
½ teaspoon nutmeg
½ teaspoon salt
2 tablespoons ice water

Filling:
½ pound sharp cheddar cheese, grated
4 eggs, well beaten
¼ teaspoon salt
¼ teaspoon cayenne pepper

Heat oven to 400 degrees. Place flour, butter, nutmeg and salt in a medium bowl and cut in butter with a pastry blender until mixture

Photographed by Francis P. Johnson in 1959, these *fromajardis* are traditional Minorcan pastries filled with cheese. The leftover dough is sprinkled with cinnamon sugar and baked as a crispy snack.

resembles coarse cornmeal. Sprinkle with ice water, tossing lightly with a fork until moistened and beginning to clump together. Form into a ball. Refrigerate at least 1 hour. On lightly floured surface, roll out pastry to $\frac{1}{8}$-inch thickness. Use a 3- to 6-inch cookie cutter to cut circles from the dough. Cut a cross shape into one side of each circle of dough. Combine cheese, eggs, salt and cayenne pepper and place a spoonful atop one half of each circle on the uncut side. Fold over the cheese mixture to make half-moon shapes, with the cross on top. Pinch edges together with moistened fingers and crimp with a fork. Bake on greased baking sheet until cheese begins to ooze out the cut-cross and pastry is golden brown, or 18–20 minutes.

The Minorcans are not only known for their extremely hot Datil peppers, but they were also avid mullet fishermen and might have been the first to stir a little mayonnaise into their smoked mullet to create a Florida favorite, smoked fish dip. In the mid-1700s, when the Duke of Richelieu arrived in Minorca, at the port city of Mahan, mayonnaise was created from eggs and oil for a banquet. Today, smoking meat and fish is a flavor enhancer, and the food should be eaten or refrigerated shortly after it's smoked. Mullet and mackerel are great for smoking due to their high fat content. Ted Peter's Famous Smoked Fish, in the Saint Petersburg area, has mastered the art of smoking fish, serving it for over fifty years.

Easy Smoked Fish Dip

½ pound smoked mullet, skin and bones removed
½ cup mayonnaise
½ cup sour cream
1 lemon, juiced
1 teaspoon grated onion
½ teaspoon salt
¼ teaspoon Datil pepper sauce

Combine all ingredients and chill before serving with crackers.

Orange Broiled Grouper

William Bartram, in Travels and Other Writings *(1791), described the broiled fish he prepared for himself while exploring the flora and fauna of Florida. It sounds like gourmet dining by today's standards. It was freshly caught fish, cleaned and broiled, served over a bed of rice with a drizzle of wild, sour Florida orange juice. Combining orange and lemon juice mimics the taste of sour orange and can be drizzled over fish with olive oil before broiling or grilling. Cooking the fish ten minutes per inch of thickness is recommended; if the fish flakes easily with a fork, it's done.*

FROM SWAMP CABBAGE TO SYLLABUB

Native Americans introduced settlers to roots, berries, nuts, wild plants and tropical fruits such as mangos, bananas and coconuts. B.F. French explained in *Historical Collections of Louisiana and Florida*, "the Southern Indians were, in general, great gourmands and lived sumptuously on wild game, fish, and oysters, buffalo, deer and bear-meat in their season. They also freely ate corn, beans, pumpkins, and persimmons, of which they made bread mixed with corn-meal." Seminoles laid the foundation for designing a workable living arrangement with separate areas for refuse, for smoking and drying meat on racks, for earth ovens and shallow hearths for cooking and for sleeping and socializing. They also showed the homesteaders new foods as a link to survival, such as the coontie, prickly pear cactus, swamp cabbage and poke salad.

Swamp cabbage, frog legs and fried gator have survived through the ages with the help of Seminole and Cracker cooking. High in protein and low in cholesterol, the alligator is now farm-raised in Florida. Like the pig, there is little waste when butchered. Frog legs are still served today in many restaurants around the state, but it's usually the swamp cabbage that garners the most attention. The small town of LaBelle, located between Fort Myers and Lake Okeechobee, is home to the annual Swamp Cabbage Festival. It's held right down the road from "The Redneck Yacht Club," a muddy field full of people, pick-up trucks, beer and fun. Also known as hearts of palm in many gourmet restaurants, swamp cabbage is more of a side dish in Cracker kitchens.

Southern cooking is the original American cuisine, with hundreds of books written on the subject and thousands of recipes, but it can be described with two words: comfort food. Seminole, southern, soul and Cracker cooking are all rooted in the past, with a common thread of freshly picked or harvested fruits and vegetables; fish and shellfish found in the myriad lakes, streams and coastal waterways; barnyard chickens, wild hogs and venison; basic cooking skills; and a taste that is recognizably the South with seasonal treats such as cane syrup, boiled peanuts, muscadine grapes and tupelo honey.

Colonial cookbooks introduced us to fools, shrubs and bubs. Orange juice, eggs, cream, sugar and spices are combined, heated and then cooled to make an orange-fool. A shrub is made from spirits and juice with a little spice and sugar. The syllabub, or "bub" for bubbling drink, started with milking a cow straight into a bucket of cider or wine, also known as "sillery," to create a bubbling or frothy effect. Later, a new method was introduced using a "ventilator," or whisk, to combine the milk and cider or wine. The following is an updated version. While the drink dates back to the 1600s, when it was made with a hard cider or wine, this new version introduces crisp apple cider to create a family beverage.

Syllabub

3 cups fresh apple cider
½ cup sugar
Pinch of salt
2 cups heavy cream, whipped
1 whole nutmeg, for garnish

In a saucepan, combine cider, sugar and salt. While stirring, heat the apple cider just enough to dissolve sugar and salt. Chill. In a large punch bowl, fold the whipped cream into chilled cider mixture and then whisk until frothy and combined. Sprinkle with freshly grated nutmeg before serving.

BISCUITS WERE ON THE RISE

Before baking powder was widely used, beaten biscuits on the plantation were considered an upper-class status symbol due to the excessive labor and time necessary to incorporate enough air and lightness into the dough. Using a rolling pin, mallet or the side of an axe, the dough was beaten hundreds of times on a biscuit block, taking fifteen minutes to hours until it was glossy and "blistered" with air bubbles. These flat, round, firm, dry biscuits had a texture like a crisp but chewy soda cracker. By the 1900s, wheat flour was common, but soft, low-gluten southern flour is needed to make great southern biscuits. At first, baking powder was considered dangerous, for fear it could explode, but once it was accepted, the southern biscuit was on the rise. In 1930, General Mills introduced Bisquick and refrigerated unbaked stacks of biscuits in pop-open cardboard tubes. Self-rising flour made the process one step easier, and by the 1960s, crescent rolls and the Pillsbury Doughboy were popular. Most of the work was already done—mixing bowls, measuring cups and flour-covered pastry boards were no longer needed. The chemical reaction of buttermilk and soda is the magic that makes these biscuits rise. A substitute for buttermilk is to add a little vinegar to whole milk, but the buttermilk is so much better.

GrandMary's Buttermilk Biscuits

2 cups flour
1 tablespoon baking powder
½ teaspoon baking soda
¼ teaspoon salt
½ cup (8 tablespoons) butter, chilled and cut into 6 pieces
¾–1 cup buttermilk, as needed

Heat oven to 450 degrees. Whisk together flour, baking powder, baking soda and salt. Cut in butter with a pastry blender until mixture resembles coarse crumbs. Stir in ¾ cup buttermilk with a fork (stir in more if needed to moisten dough). Stir lightly and rapidly until a soft, non-sticky dough forms, being careful not to over mix. Knead on a lightly floured surface 3–4 times and then roll dough or pat to ½-inch thickness. Cut with a 2- to 3-inch biscuit

Homegrown sugarcane was used to make Florida cane syrup on many homesteads across the state, as shown in this 1947 Citrus County photograph.

cutter. Place in a cast-iron skillet and bake for 14 minutes, or until tops are lightly golden. Serve with sausage gravy, honey butter, Florida cane syrup or mayhaw jelly. Mayhaw jelly is a springtime treat and can sometimes be purchased from roadside stands along the back roads of Florida. Florida cane syrup can usually be found year-round, along the road or stocked on the shelves of country stores. Homemade sausage is another southern treat, and written recipes appear in some of the first cookbooks published. It's a simple combination of fresh, lean pork chopped fine with added spices such as salt, pepper and sage.

Sausage Gravy

6 ounces ground pork sausage
2 tablespoons butter
¼ cup flour
1½ cups whole milk
½ teaspoon salt
½ teaspoon pepper
Sage, to taste

Crumble and cook sausage in a large skillet over medium heat, until it is no longer pink. Remove sausage with a slotted spoon and drain on a paper towel. Melt butter in skillet with sausage drippings over low heat. Whisk in flour and stir for 3 minutes, until light brown, like a roux. Whisk in milk, salt, pepper and sage. Cook over medium heat until thickened and bubbly, about 1 minute more. Stir in crumbled sausage. Serve over biscuits.

Orange Blossom Honey Butter

You may use any flavor honey, tupelo, mangrove, sea grape or gallberry, since the orange flavor comes from the zest. The fame of tupelo honey is that it doesn't crystallize. Placing a jar in warm water or in a sunny location can liquefy crystallized honey. North Florida Native Americans, along with roadside vendors in the Panhandle, collect and sell honey. The Harold P. Curtis Honey Company, next to Bridge Street in LaBelle, is home to another popular beekeeper selling a variety of honey and honey products since 1921.

½ cup (8 tablespoons) butter, softened
¼ cup honey
½ teaspoon orange zest
Pinch of salt

Mix all ingredients together until thoroughly blended, or whip until light and fluffy. Chill. Use on biscuits, waffles, pancakes, quick breads and baked sweet potatoes.

PIGS AND PONE

Charles Lamb, in his humorous essay "A Dissertation on Roast Pig," tells a fictional account of discovering roasted pig when a young boy accidentally caused a fire that burned down the family home with piglets trapped inside. As the aroma wafted through town, the boy found the charred piglets and, after touching them, licked his fingers and "for the first time in his life… tasted crackling." Bacon and bacon drippings are such an integral part of southern cooking that many remember a grease canister placed upon the stovetop to store the drippings after frying up a batch of bacon in the morning—this was then used to season vegetables, cornbread or other dishes throughout the day. Recipes for making bacon appear in some of the first cookbooks available. In the early 1800s, Hannah Glasse and Mary Randolph gave detailed descriptions of the process in their cookbooks, but unless you have a smokehouse, you might want to peruse the markets and find your own favorite brand.

Native Americans, who baked, dried and pounded corn mixed with water and salt on hot stones, introduced pone. Later, the same combination of ingredients was baked on the back of a hoe or a utensil made specifically for hoecakes. Today, the hoecake is a quick and simple bread to make: with 1 cup corn meal and ¾ cup hot water, stirred together with a little salt, small amounts are then cooked on a hot cast-iron skillet with a little bacon grease.

No Florida fish fry would be complete without hush puppies and cheese grits on the menu. According to legend, hush puppies were so named because they were used to quiet the barking dogs in Saint Marks. Similar to corn bread (with chopped onion added and fried instead of baked), hush puppies are made by dropping spoonfuls of dough into hot grease and are one of the most popular classic Cracker foods.

Cheese grits can be as easy as stirring your favorite cheese into a bowl of warm cooked grits or by also stirring in an egg and ham and then baking them in the oven. Old-fashioned coarse grits, such as the ones sold at Bradley's Country Store near Tallahassee, require a longer cooking time than most varieties found at the local grocery store. Bradley's Country Store, on the National Register of Historic Places, has been selling smoked sausage, cornmeal and stone-ground grits since the 1920s.

Homemade Corn Chips

1 cup fine (white, stone-ground) corn meal
1–1½ cups boiling water
3 tablespoons butter, melted
½ teaspoon salt
Corn oil

Heat oven to 350 degrees. Stir boiling water into cornmeal until smooth, using only enough water for a thick batter. Stir in butter and salt. Pour into greased cast-iron skillet and bake in oven for 45 minutes. Remove from oven and cut into 1-inch by 1-inch strips. Heat skillet with ½ inch of corn oil on the stovetop. Add strips a few at a time to hot skillet and cook until crisp. Drain on paper towels.

FRICASSEED, FRIED, PERLOO AND PIE

Recipes for fricasseed or stewed chicken can be found in early American cookbooks, but southern fried chicken is the dish most often associated with the South, and for good reason. Brillat-Savarin, in 1825, recognized the greatness of all things fried in one of his Meditations. In *The Physiology of Taste*, he attested that "fried things are highly popular at any celebration: they add a piquant variety to any menu," adding that the secret of good frying on high heat creates "a little package of food encased in a delicious crust." When preparing chicken dishes, use an old, fat hen for stewing and a young, lean chicken for frying. When frying, chicken will not cook properly if the skillet is overcrowded. Perloos and pies are still a big part of chicken dishes served across the state. A perloo comes in many versions and combinations, but the combination of rice and chicken on Cracker homesteads was made to feed large groups of people with very little chicken.

Cast-Iron Skillet Chicken Pie

½ cup chopped Florida sweet onion
½ cup chopped celery
½ cup chopped carrot
¼ cup (4 tablespoons) butter
⅓ cup flour
1½ teaspoons salt
½ teaspoon white pepper
2½ cups chicken stock
½ cup heavy cream
2 cups chicken, cooked and chopped
1 cup fresh or frozen peas
9-inch pastry

Heat oven to 450 degrees. In a cast-iron skillet, sauté onion, celery and carrot in butter over medium heat. Stir in flour, salt and pepper; cook 2–3 minutes while stirring. Gradually stir in chicken stock and cream. Continue cooking and stirring occasionally until thick, 20–25 minutes. Add chicken and peas and then heat to bubbling. Place pastry over chicken mixture and bake in oven for 15 minutes, or until the pastry is golden brown.

Turn of the Century to Turn of the Century

Steamboats, railroads and the automobile brought tourism to the Sunshine State. Backyard gardens grew into large-scale farms. "Shoot-and-Serve" would no longer be the mantra for dining in or out, as the food choices grew every day. The modern era of fine dining and the casual roadside cafés were serving a combination of foods from distinctly different cultures, creating entirely new dishes. Grocery stores with brand-name products made cooking at home easier than ever. The transformation of recipes from using all homegrown ingredients to gourmet delights purchased at the market had a big impact on Florida cooking. With southern gems like Coca-Cola, Pepsi, RC Cola and Nehi, it's no wonder "sweet tea is the house wine of the South." Still, two other Florida creations had a major impact on national beverage consumption. Gatorade was created as a sports drink for rehydration of athletes at the University of Florida, and in the late 1940s, frozen, concentrated orange juice was developed for the U.S. government for shipment to troops fighting overseas. This changed the look of the breakfast table across the country. Florida orange juice is now associated with a typical American breakfast.

Coconut Macaroons

The path of the Gilded Age macaroon is a long and winding one, as this concoction started out as almond based and today is considered a coconut delight. Almonds were used after they had been dried and pounded to a powder. "Grated cocoanut may be substituted for almonds," appeared at the end of the recipe in Mrs. Hill's New Cook Book *in 1870. The* Dixie Cook-Book, *by Estelle Woods Wilcox, shared confectionery tips in 1883: "In baking macaroons and kisses, use washed butter for greasing the tins, as lard or salt butter gives an unpleasant taste…In making Macaroons or drops, or pulling butter-scotch or taffy, grease hands lightly with butter to prevent sticking." Coconuts are not indigenous to Florida; they first arrived in the late 1800s, by way of a shipwreck off the southeast coast. This white, flaky taste of heaven has been a favorite among Floridians ever since. An additional note on working with coconut: When a recipe calls for coconut milk, it is not describing the watery liquid found inside a fresh coconut but a canned product found on grocery shelves.*

1½ cups flaked coconut
⅓ cup sugar
2 egg whites
2 tablespoons flour
½ teaspoon almond or vanilla extract
⅛ teaspoon salt

Heat oven to 325 degrees. Combine all ingredients, mixing well. Drop by spoonful onto buttered parchment paper. Bake in oven for 25 minutes or until golden brown on the edges. Cool. These do not store well and should be eaten right away.

Oranges were preserved in kegs of rum in early Saint Augustine or eaten freshly plucked from the tree, as George M. Barbour described to newcomers in 1882: "Now, gentlemen, roll up your sleeves, remove your cuffs, high collars, etc…take a sharp knife, pull a dark-shade, heavy orange, peel it to the quick all around, leave no bitter rind, shut your eyes and suck; don't bite—just suck." Another great way to enjoy citrus in Florida is in baked goods: candy, cakes, cookies and savory dishes as well. There are recipes for Florida grapefruit cake and ambrosia cake, but my favorite is the orange cake. Baking a cake has become simplified and no longer requires collecting eggs from the henhouse, churning butter, scraping sugar, milking the cow and feeding the fire. The time-consuming cooked egg-white frosting has been replaced with an easy orange chocolate chip frosting, and cupcakes make the process fast and simple.

Orange Chocolate Chip Cupcakes

2 ½ cups flour
2 ½ teaspoons baking powder
½ teaspoon salt
⅔ cup butter, at room temperature
1¾ cups sugar
2 teaspoons vanilla
2 eggs
1¼ cups whole milk
1 cup mini chocolate chips
2 teaspoons orange zest
Orange chip frosting (see recipe)

Heat oven to 350 degrees. Line muffin tin with cupcake papers. Whisk together flour, baking powder and salt; set aside. Cream together butter and sugar; stir in vanilla. Add eggs, one at time, beating well after each addition. Alternately add flour mixture and milk, beating after each addition until combined. Stir in chips and zest. Spoon into muffin tin. Bake 20–25 minutes. Cool in pan 10 minutes. Remove from pan and completely cool on rack before frosting.

Orange Chip Frosting

⅓ cup butter at room temperature
3¾ cups confectioners sugar, divided
2 tablespoons milk
2 tablespoons orange juice
2 teaspoons vanilla
2 teaspoons orange zest
½ cup mini chocolate chips

Beat butter and 2 cups sugar together. Stir in milk and beat in orange juice and vanilla. Beat in remaining sugar. Stir in zest and chips.

Holiday Ambrosia

The holiday season is a time to bring on all the rich, delicious desserts, but the citrus combination of chilled orange sections with coconut and sugar would be missed if it didn't grace the festive dinner table in many traditional southern homes.

ROADSIDE MARKETS

While driving through North Florida and the heartland, for a taste of Old Florida you can pick up native foods at roadside stands such as boiled peanuts, peanut brittle, sugared pecans and a variety of honey, from tupelo to gallberry. In the springtime, there is mayhaw jelly, and the fall brings in a new batch of Florida cane syrup and, now, year-round boiled peanuts. At one time, boiled peanuts were a seasonal treat, but they are so popular in North Florida that peanut farmers freeze the early season green peanuts so they can be boiled any time of year. The peanut-picking machine reduced the labor-intensive work for peanut famers. As the machine crawls down each row, the vines are lifted into a hopper. Boiled, roasted and even fried, the majority of peanuts are dried, shelled and processed into peanut butter. Peanut butter was created in 1890 to provide a nutritious, easily digestible food for the elderly. Raw shelled peanuts can be roasted on a shallow pan in a single layer at 350 degrees for 30 to 45 minutes. Boiled peanuts are made from the first green nuts pulled from the ground before they are fully ripened.

Preston Bozeman has been selling Owens tupelo honey at this intersection in northwest Florida for years. A few of the other items sold by roadside vendors include mayhaw jelly, pecans, boiled peanuts and Florida cane syrup. *Photographed by Joy Sheffield Harris.*

Grand Floyd's Boiled Peanuts

3 pounds young green peanuts, in the shell
3 tablespoons salt

Wash the peanuts in the shell under cool running water. Place peanuts in a large pot and add enough water to cover. Add approximately 1 tablespoon salt for each quart of water. Bring to a boil; reduce heat to medium and continue to simmer rapidly. Cook 2½–3 hours, adding water as needed. Allow peanuts to sit in the pot to absorb desired amount of salt. Remove the shell before eating.

CAFETERIA CANDY

School lunches in North Florida were probably some of the best in the country. Class favorites included yeast rolls, chess pie, cinnamon rolls, éclairs, fried chicken, shrimp creole, beef tips, gravy with mashed potatoes, chili and grilled cheese sandwiches. Brownies, with peanut butter stirred into the batter before baking, were a common dessert. The most popular was most likely the peanut butter bars.

Peanut Butter Bars

2 cups graham cracker crumbs
1 cup creamy peanut butter
⅓ cup melted butter
1 cup powdered sugar, divided

Combine all ingredients, reserving ¼ cup of powdered sugar. Press into a 9-inch by 9-inch pan. Sprinkle with remaining powdered sugar.

WILD FLORIDA SEAFOOD

From the time the Archaic fisherman first caught a fish with his bare hands to the aquaculture farming of today, the cooking methods are basic but the recipes endless. Saint Joseph Bay and Steinhatchee scallops are plentiful and easy to catch during scallop season. Whether you wade out or snorkel along and scoop them up, once they are cleaned, cooking them is easy as well. While working for the Florida Department of Natural Resources, I created a scallop chowder recipe for our cookbook *Southern Seafood Classics*. Stir a couple pounds of tiny scallops into cooked potato chowder and heat until scallops are fully cooked, or until they turn from translucent to milky white. Sometimes it's the sauce that makes the dish, but with Florida seafood, it's the combination of the two. With the emerald-green waters of the Gulf of Mexico lapping at the entire west and south coastline of Florida and the Atlantic Ocean running along the north to southeast coast, fresh seafood is never far away.

Stone Crab Claw Hot Mustard Sauce

The large black-tipped claw is snapped off, and the crab is returned alive to the water to regenerate a replacement. They are usually cooked and frozen on the boat to capture the freshness.

½ cup sour cream
2 tablespoons yellow mustard
2 teaspoons butter, melted
⅛ teaspoon salt

Combine all ingredients and heat until warm.

Florida Cocktail Sauce

Oysters take on the flavor of the area they are from, and the Apalachicola Bay oysters are some of the best in the world. Still, shrimp seems to be the most popular shellfish in Florida.

½ cup chili sauce
½ cup catsup
3 tablespoons lemon or lime juice
1 tablespoon horseradish
1 teaspoon Worcestershire sauce
½ teaspoon grated onion
Dash of Datil hot pepper sauce
Salt and pepper, to taste

Combine all ingredients and chill.

REGIONAL RECIPES

The iconic Cuban sandwich has been dubbed the state sandwich of Florida, with a battle going on between Tampa and Miami to claim the origin of this notable combination of meats, cheese and Cuban bread.

It's found in fancy restaurants, sandwich shops and convenience stores, but to properly prepare one, you must use Cuban bread and press the sandwich when assembled. Here is the version I learned while attending a workshop on Cuban sandwiches at the state's oldest restaurant, the Columbia Restaurant in Tampa. They have been using Cuban bread from La Segunda Central Bakery since 1915. Each loaf is topped with a palm frond to aid in baking, an element grandfathered into the federal food-service regulations.

Cuban Sandwich

1 9-inch piece of Cuban bread
1 tablespoon yellow mustard
4 ounces glazed ham, thinly sliced
1½ ounces Cuban pork, roasted
1 ounce genoa salami, thinly sliced
1 ounce swiss cheese, thinly sliced
2 long pieces sliced dill pickle
1 teaspoon butter

Slice the Cuban bread lengthwise and spread mustard on the top half. Layer ham, pork, salami, cheese and dill pickles on the bottom half. Put the two halves together and brush both top and bottom with butter before pressing. If you don't have a traditional sandwich press, you can improvise by placing the sandwich in a heated skillet and pressing it with the bottom of a heated Dutch oven. Cut diagonally before serving.

You can also make a great-tasting cup of café con leche at home with steamed milk and a bold Cuban coffee such as Café Bustelo, Pilon or Naviera Coffee. Prepare a shot of espresso and stir in at least an equal amount of steamed milk. If you don't have a milk steamer, just heat the amount of whole milk you will need in the microwave until almost boiling. Add sugar to taste. Serve with buttered Cuban toast for a light breakfast.

SALMAGUNDI

Recipes for salmagundi, a type of layer salad, appeared in colonial cookbooks, leading the way to culinary exploration of a variety of flavors and textures combined in one bowl to create a meal in itself. With chopped meats, anchovies, eggs, greens and other vegetables arranged in rows or rings within the salad bowl for contrast, the salad was served with a lemon or butter dressing. Louis M. Pappamichalopoulos, who shortened his name to Pappas shortly after arriving in America, created his now famous version of the Greek salad by adding a scoop of potato salad to the bottom of the bowl. His salad is dressed with distilled white vinegar, olive oil and oregano. Today, the humble café that started in 1925 in Tarpon Springs has developed into a chain of restaurants called Louis Pappas Fresh Greek, serving the popular salad with other Greek specialties.

Louis Pappas created his famous Greek salad in Tarpon Springs. Here he is with his son Michael in 1947. *Photographed by Joseph Janney Steinmetz.*

Little Greek Salad

Large or small, it's up to you. Here is my version of that famous Greek salad.

Potato salad
Romaine lettuce, chopped
Tomatoes, seeded and chopped
Cucumber, seeded, peeled and chopped
Radish, grated
Kalamata olives
Beets, chopped
Feta cheese, crumbled
Anchovies (optional)
Shrimp, cooked (optional)

Put a scoop of your favorite potato salad in the bottom of a salad bowl before topping it with romaine lettuce, chopped tomatoes, cucumber, radish, kalamata olives, beets and feta cheese. Top with anchovies and cooked shrimp, if desired.

Easy Greek Dressing

¾ cup white vinegar
2 tablespoons olive oil
2 tablespoons vegetable oil
I teaspoon dried oregano

Combine all ingredients in a jar with a tight-fitting lid and shake well.

Honey Orange Railway Salad Dressing

The East Coast Restaurant at the East Coast Railway Station in New Smyrna had no menu but featured a house salad dressing using orange juice. Here is my version of honey orange dressing to use on a tossed salad.

¼ cup Florida orange juice
¼ cup honey

¼ cup white vinegar

½ cup vegetable oil

I teaspoon grated onion

¼ teaspoon sea salt

⅛ teaspoon white pepper

Combine all ingredients in a jar with a tight-fitting lid and shake well. Refrigerated, it will keeps for weeks.

Special 1905 Salad Dressing

The nationally known 1905 Salad from the Columbia Restaurant is a combination of iceberg lettuce, tomato, julienned ham, swiss cheese, green spanish olive, grated romano cheese and a special 1905 dressing. Here is my version of this special dressing.

2 tablespoons extra-virgin olive oil

2 tablespoons salad oil

2 tablespoons Worcestershire sauce

2 tablespoons white wine vinegar

4 cloves garlic, minced

I teaspoon freshly squeezed lemon juice

Combine all ingredients in a jar with a tight-fitting lid and shake well.

THE STATE PIE OF FLORIDA

The archipelago of the Florida Keys is nestled where the Gulf of Mexico and Atlantic Ocean come together to make up the waterways of the Keys. This area serves up Caribbean- and Cuban-inspired dishes, along with grouper, spiny lobster, conch fritters, chowder, avocado, plantains, guava, papaya, pineapple, coconut and—most importantly—the state pie of Florida, Key lime pie. Key limes are smaller, thin-skinned and more perishable than Persian limes but also more tart and aromatic. Key limes are the same as the Mexican or West Indian limes sold in many markets today. If you need to substitute a larger Persian lime, use one for every three Key limes.

Gail Borden accidently discovered that adding sugar to milk increases the shelf life, making it a popular choice for troops at military camps. The combination of Key limes and sweetened condensed milk for Key lime pie might have been accidental as well, because fishermen brought Key limes and canned milk on their fishing trips.

The popularity of Gail Borden's sweetened condensed milk began after it was shipped to troops during the Civil War. Preserving the milk by adding sugar gave the product stability and was the catalyst that propelled the Key lime pie to culinary fame. This simple concoction of sweetened condensed milk, egg and Key lime juice is truly a masterpiece of confectionary perfection. The pie is usually topped with golden-brown meringue made from egg whites, while their yolks are in the yellow filling. At one time, many tourist-oriented places added a little green food coloring for visual appeal, since the natural color of the pie is a dull yellow. A simple pastry or graham crackers makes up the crust. Many versions of the original are in cookbooks and on menus across the state. Here is mine.

Creamy Coconut-Crusted Key Lime Pie

⅓ cup cream cheese, softened
1 egg
1 (14-ounce) can sweetened condensed milk
½ cup Key lime juice (10–12 Key limes)
9-inch coconut graham crust (see recipe)
Kahlúa whipped cream (see recipe)

Heat oven to 325 degrees. In a medium bowl, beat the cream cheese until smooth and creamy; then beat in egg, milk and lime juice. Pour into prepared crust and spread evenly. Bake for 15 minutes. Remove from oven and chill 5–6 hours before topping with whipped cream.

Coconut Graham Crust

½ cup flaked coconut
1 cup graham cracker crumbs
¼ cup sugar
⅓ cup melted butter

Heat oven to 350 degrees. Combine all ingredients and mix well. Press mixture evenly into a 9-inch pie plate. Bake in oven for 5 minutes. Remove from oven and cool.

Kahlúa Whipped Cream

1 cup heavy cream
1 tablespoon sugar
1 teaspoon Kahlúa

In a chilled bowl, beat heavy cream until it forms soft peaks; sprinkle sugar over the cream and beat until it forms stiff peaks. Fold in Kahlúa.

Bibliography

BOOKS

Andersen, Lars. *Paynes Prairie*. Sarasota, FL: Pineapple Press, 2010.

Barbour, George M. *Florida for Tourists, Invalids, and Settlers*. A facsimile reproduction of the 1882 edition.

Bartram, William. *Travels and Other Writings*. 1791. Reprint, New York: Penguin Books, 1996.

Bass, Bob. *When Steamboats Reigned in Florida*. Gainesville: University Press of Florida, 2008.

Beecher, Catherine Esther. *A Treatise on Domestic Economy*. 1845. Biblio Bazaar, 2008.

Beeson, Kenneth H, Jr. *Fromajadas and Indigo*. Charleston, SC: The History Press, 2006.

Braden, Susan R. *The Architecture of Leisure*. Gainesville: University Press of Florida, 2002.

Brillat-Savarin, Jean Anthelme. *The Physiology of Taste: Or Meditations on Transcendental Gastronomy*. 1826. Translated by M.F.K. Fisher. New York: Alfred A. Knopf, 1971.

Brown, Robin C. *Florida's First People*. Sarasota, FL: Pineapple Press, 1994.

Bushnell, Amy. *The King's Coffer*. Gainesville: University Press of Florida, 1981.

Byrd, Maryann. *The Rise of the Southern Biscuit*. 2006. Byrdword Productions, 2010.

Coe, Sophie. *America's First Cuisines*. Austin: University of Texas Press, 1994.

Cowan, Ruth Schwartz. *More Work for Mother: The Ironies of Household Technology from the Open Hearth to the Microwave*. New York: Basic Books, Inc., 1983.

Cresap, Ida Keeling. *The History of Florida Agriculture: The Early Era*. Electronic version. Gainesville, 2001.

Crosby, Alfred W., Jr. *The Columbian Exchange*. Westport, CT: Greenwood Press, 1973.

Davies, Frederick S., and Larry K. Jackson. *Citrus Growing in Florida*. Gainesville: University Press of Florida, 2009.

Deuerling, Richard J., and Peggy S. Lantz. *Florida's Incredible Wild Edibles*. Orlando: The Florida Native Plant Society, 2000.

Dickinson, Jonathan. *Jonathan Dickinson's Journal, or Gods Protecting Providence, Being the Narrative of a Journey from Port Royal in Jamaica to Philadelphia, August 23, 1696 to April 1st, 1697*. Edited by E.W. Andrews and C.M. Andrews. Port Salerno: Florida Classic Library, 1985.

Doran, Glen H., ed. *Windover Multidisciplinary Investigations of an Early Archaic Florida Cemetery*. Gainesville: University Press of Florida, 2002.

Eden, Trudy. *Cooking in America 1590–1840*. Westport, CT: Greenwood Press, 2006.

Edge, John T. *A Gracious Plenty: Recipes and Recollections from the American South*. New York: Penguin Putnam, 1999.

Egerton, John. *Southern Food: At Home, on the Road, in History*. Chapel Hill: University of North Carolina Press, 1993.

Eppes, Susan Bradford. *Through Some Eventful Years*. A facsimile reproduction of the 1926 edition.

Fairbanks, George R. *History of Florida*. A facsimile reproduction of the 1871 edition.

———. *The Spaniards in Florida*. A facsimile reproduction of the 1868 edition.

Fernandez-Armesto, Felipe. *Food: A History*. London: Macmillan, 2001.

Fishburne, Charles Carroll, Jr. *The Cedar Keys in the 19th Century*. Cedar Key, FL: Cedar Key Historical Society, 2004.

Ford, Richard I., ed. *Prehistoric Food Production in North America*. Ann Arbor: University of Michigan Press, 1985.

French, B.F. *Historical Collections of Louisiana and Florida*. A facsimile reproduction of the 1882 edition.

Fussell, Betty. *The Story of Corn*. New York: Knopf, 1992.

Gannon, Michael. *The Cross in the Sand: The Early Catholic Church in Florida, 1513–1870*. Gainesville: University Press of Florida, 1993.

———. *Michael Gannon's History of Florida in 40 Minutes*. Gainesville: University Press of Florida, 2007.

Gould, Mary Earle. *Early American Wooden Ware & Other Kitchen Utensils*. A facsimile reproduction of the 1942 edition.

Green, Mary Fulford, and Linda Molto. *Cortez—Then and Now*. Cortez, FL: Cortez Village Historical Society, 1997.

Griffin, Patricia C. *Mullet on the Beach: The Minorcans of Florida 1768–1788*. Jacksonville: University of North Florida Press, 1991.

Haber, Barbara. *From Hardtack to Home Fries: An Uncommon History of American Cooks and Meals*. New York: Free Press, 2003.

Hann, John H., and Bonnie G. McEwan. *The Apalachee Indians and Mission San Luis*. Gainesville: University Press of Florida, 1998.

Harland, Marion. *Common Sense in the Household: A Manual of Practical Housewifery*. A facsimile reproduction of the 1880 edition.

Hess, John L., and Karen Hess. *The Taste of America*. Chicago: University of Illinois Press, 2000.

Hilliard, Sam Bowers. *Hog Meat and Hoecakes: Food Supply in the Old South, 1840–1860*. Carbondale: Southern Illinois University Press, 1972.

Hines, Duncan. *Adventures in Good Eating*. 5th ed. Chicago: Adventures in Good Eating, 1938.

Josephy, Alvin M., Jr. *The Indian Heritage of America*. Boston: Houghton Mifflin, 1991.

Kavasch, E. Barrier. *Native Harvests: American Indian Wild Foods and Recipes*. Mineola, NY: Dover Publications, 2005.

Kennedy, Nancy. *The Ford Treasury of Favorite Recipes from Famous Eating Places*. New York: Simon and Schuster, 1955.

———— *The New Ford Treasury of Favorite Recipes from Famous Places*. New York: Golden Press, 1966.

————. *The Second Ford Treasury of Favorite Recipes from Famous Eating Places*. New York: Simon and Schuster, 1954.

Kurlansky, Mark. *The Food of a Younger Land*. New York: Penguin, 2009.

Lamb, Charles. *A Dissertation on Roast Pig and Other Essays*. New York: Penguin, 2011.

Larson, Lewis H. *Aboriginal Subsistence Technology on the Southeastern Coastal Plain during the Late Prehistoric Period*. Gainesville: University Press of Florida, 1980.

Laszlo, Pierre. *Citrus: A History*. Chicago: University of Chicago Press, 2007.

Lee, Harper. *To Kill a Mockingbird*. New York: J.P. Lippincott Company, 1962.

Lowenstein, Eleanor. *American Cookery Books, 1742–1860*. New York: American Antiquarian Society, 1972.

MacMahon, Darcie A., and William H. Marquardt. *The Calusa and Their Legacy*. Gainesville: University Press of Florida, 2004.

McCarthy, Kevin. *Cedar Key, Florida: A History*. Charleston, SC: The History Press, 2007.

McWhiney, Grady. *Cracker Culture: Celtic Ways in the Old South*. Tuscaloosa: University of Alabama Press, 1988

McWilliams, James E. *A Revolution in Eating*. New York: Columbia University Press, 2005.

Milanich, Jerald T. *Florida Indians and the Invasion from Europe*. Gainesville: University Press of Florida, 1995.

————. *Florida Indians from Ancient Times to the Present*. Gainesville: University Press of Florida, 1998.

————. *Life in a 9ᵗʰ-Century Indian Household: A Weeden Island Fall-Winter Site on the Upper Apalachicola River, Florida*. Divison of Archives, History and Records Management, Florida Department of State, 1974.

Perkins, Frederic Beecher. *Narrative of LeMoyne: An Artist Who Accompanied the French Expedition to Florida under Laudonniere, 1564*. A facsimile reproduction of the 1875 edition.

Perry, I. Mac. *Indian Mounds You Can Visit: 165 Aboriginal Sites of Florida's West Coast*. St. Petersburg, FL: Great Outdoors, 1998.

Pinardi, Norman J. *The Plant Pioneers: The Story of the Reasoner Family, Pioneer Florida Horticulturists and Their Nursery*. Torrington, CT: Rainbow Press, 1980.

Purdy, Barbara A. *Florida's People During the Last Ice Age*. Gainesville: University Press of Florida, 2008.

Rabinowitz, Larry. *Plants of Historic Spanish Point*. Osprey, FL: Gulf Coast Heritage Association, 1998.

Rolle, Denys. *Humble Petition*. A facsimile reproduction of the 1765 edition. Gainesville: University Press of Florida, 1977.

Romans, Bernard. *A Concise Natural History of East and West Florida*. A facsimile reproduction of the 1775 edition.

Rountree, Helen C. *The Powhatan Indians of Virginia: Their Traditional Culture*. Norman: University of Oklahoma Press, 1989.

Shaw, Hank. *Hunt, Gather, Cook: Finding the Forgotten Feast*. New York: Rodale, 2011.

Smith, Andrew F. *Eating History: 30 Turning Points in the Making of American Cuisine*. New York: Columbia University Press, 2009.

Snyder, James D. *Five Thousand Years on the Loxahatchee*. Jupiter, FL: Pharos Books, 2003.

Stage, Sarah, and Virginia B. Vincenti, eds. *Rethinking Home Economics: Women and the History of a Profession*. Ithaca, NY: Cornell University Press, 1997.

Standage, Tom. *An Edible History of Humanity*. New York: Walker and Company, 2009.

Ste. Claire, Dana. *Cracker—the Cracker Culture in Florida*. Daytona Beach, FL: Museum of Arts and Sciences, 1998.

Stowe, Harriet Beecher. *Palmetto Leaves*. 1873. Gainesville, University Press of Florida, 1999.

Symons, Michael. *A History of Cooks and Cooking*. Chicago: Illinois Press, 2004.

Tannahill, Reay. *Food in History*. New York: Three Rivers Press, 1988.

Tebeau, Charlton W. *The Story of the Chokoloskee Bay Country: With the Reminiscences of Pioneer C.S. Ted Smallwood*. Miami: Florida Flair Books, 2004.

Thayer, Samuel. *The Forager's Harvest*. Birchwood, WI: Forager's Harvest Press, 2006.

Toussaint-Samat, Maguelonne. *A History of Food*. Paris: Wiley-Blackwell, 2009.

Townshend, F. Trench. *Wild Life in Florida: With a Visit to Cuba*. 1875. Memphis: General Books, 2010.

Visser, Margaret. *The Rituals of Dinner*. New York: Penguin, 1992.

Warner, Joe G. *Biscuits and 'Taters: A History of Cattle Ranching in Manatee County*. St. Petersburg, FL: Great Outdoors, 1980.

Weaver, Brian, and Richard Weaver. *The Citrus Industry in the Sunshine State*. Charleston, SC: Arcadia Publishing, 1999.

Weitzel, Kelley G. *The Timucua Indians: A Native American Detective Story*. Gainesville: University Press of Florida, 2000.

Will, Lawrence E. *Swamp to Sugar Bowl: Pioneer Days in Belle Glade*. Belle Glade, FL: Glades Historical Society, 1984.

Wilson, Charles Reagan, and William Ferris. *Encyclopedia of Southern Culture*. Chapel Hill: University of North Carolina Press, 1989.

Wing, Elizabeth S., and Antoinette B. Brown. *Paleonutrition: Method and Theory in Prehistoric Foodways*. New York: Academic Press, 1979.

Womack, Marlene. *Along the Bay: A Pictorial History of Bay County*. Norfolk, VA: Pictorial Heritage Publishing, 1994.

Workman, Richard W. *Growing Native: Native Plants for Landscape Use in Coastal South Florida*. Sanibel, FL: Sanibel-Captiva Conservation Foundation, 1980.

Wrangham, Richard. *Catching Fire: How Cooking Made Us Human*. New York: Basic Books, 2009.

Cookbooks

American Cookery. Amelia Simmons, 1796 (Facsimile Reproductions).

The American Frugal Housewife 12th ed. Mrs. Lydia Marie Child, 1832 (Facsimile Reproductions).

The Art of Cookery Made Plain and Easy. Hannah Glasse, 1805 (Facsimile Reproductions).

Camellia Garden Circle. *Camellia Cookery: Tallahassee's Favorite Recipes*. Tallahassee, FL: Camellia Garden Circle, 1950.

Carlton, Lowis. *Famous Florida Recipes: 300 Years of Good Eating*. St. Petersburg, FL: Great Outdoors, 1972.

The Confederate Receipt Book: A Compilation of Over One Hundred Recipes Adapted to the Times. A facsimile of the 1863 edition. Antique American Cookbooks, Oxmoore House, Inc. 1985.

Dahlem, Ted. *How to Smoke Seafood Florida Cracker Style*. St. Petersburg, FL: Great Outdoors, 1971.

Dishes and Beverages of the Old South. Martha McCulloch-Williams, 1913 (Facsimile Reproductions).

The Dixie Cook-Book. Estelle Woods Wilcox, 1883 (Facsimile Reproductions).

Farmer, Fannie Merrit. *The Boston Cooking-School Cook Book*. 8th ed. New York: Little Brown, 1948.

Fisher, Abby. *What Mrs. Fisher Knows About Old Southern Cooking*. 1881. Historical notes by Karen Hess. Carlisle, MA: Applewood Books, 1995.

The Florida Tropical Cookbook. The First Presbyterian Church Miami, 1912 (Facsimile Reproductions).

The Frugal Housewife, or Complete Woman Cook. Susannah Carter, 1792 (Facsimile Reproductions).

Hall, Maggi Smith. *Flavors of St. Augustine: An Historic Cookbook*. St. Augustine, FL: Tailored Tours, 1999.

Hendry County Cattlewomen. *Original and Family Favorites, Volume 2*. Lenexa, KS: Cookbook Productions, 1994.

Hess, Karen, ed. *Martha Washington's Booke of Cookery and Booke of Sweetmeats, 1749*. New York: Columbia University Press, 1981.

Junior League of Tampa. *The Gasparilla Cookbook*. Tampa, FL: Favorite Recipes, 1961.

Junior Service League of Panama City. *Bay Leaves*. Panama City, FL: Cookbook Marketplace, 1975.

Kimball, Marie. *The Martha Washington Cook Book*. 6th edition. Greensville, MS: Lillie Ross Productions, 2004.

Mrs. Beeton's Book of Cookery and Household Management (1861). UK: Ward Lock, 1992.

Mrs. Hill's New Cook Book: Housekeeping Made Easy—A Practical System for Private Families, in Town and Country. A facsimile of the 1875 edtion. Antique American Cookbooks, Oxmoore House, Inc., 1985.

Nickerson, Jane. *Jane Nickerson's Florida Cookbook*. Gainesville: University Press of Florida, 1984.

Rawlings, Marjorie Kinnan. *Cross Creek Cookery*. Lady Lake, FL: Fireside Publications, 1996.

Raymond, Dorothy. *Catch and Cook Shellfish*. St. Petersburg, FL: Great Outdoors, 1973.

The Virginia Housewife, or Methodical Cook. Mary Randolph, 1824 (Facsimile Reproductions).

What's Cookin'. Bruce Women's Club and Muscogee Nation of Florida, 2007.

Wickham, John Adams. *Food Favorites of St. Augustine*. St. Augustine, FL: Historic Print and Map, 1973.

Index

About the Author

J oy Sheffield Harris was born in Tripoli, Libya, on Wheelus Field Air Force Base but moved to Florida just in time to attend Humpty Dumpty Kindergarten and, later, Florida State University. She was a home economics and history teacher and a marketing specialist for both the Florida Department of Natural Resources and the Florida Poultry Federation. Joy met her husband, Jack, while promoting Florida's natural bounty on television in the early '80s. After they were married, they briefly owned a restaurant with friends, called Harris and Company, and in 2010 they co-wrote *Easy Breezy Florida Cooking*. Their son, Jackson, traveled with them as they journeyed around the state exploring the heritage of Florida foods.